Masaru Edmund Nakawatase
246 West Upsal Street
A 101
Philadelphia   PA 19119

D1519734

American Awakening

Evolutionary Spirituality, Non-Duality, and Free
Thinking in the Tradition of American Philosophy

AMERICAN AWAKENING

EVOLUTIONARY SPIRITUALITY, NON-DUALITY, AND FREE

THINKING IN THE TRADITION OF AMERICAN PHILOSOPHY

by JEFF CARREIRA

Nature is intricate, overlapped, interweaved, and endless.

— RALPH WALDO EMERSON

AMERICAN AWAKENING

Evolutionary Spirituality, Non-Duality, and Free Thinking
in the Tradition of American Philosophy

ISBN: 978-1-7346284-9-4

Emergence Education Press
P.O. Box 63767, Philadelphia, PA 19147
www.EmergenceEducation.com

Cover and interior design by Silvia Rodrigues
Cover photo by Nicole Armitt Photography

My appreciation to Ariela Cohen for her editorial support.

CONTENTS

Reading Jeff Carreira's American Awakening sent me to my bookcase. It has been a while since I pulled out the texts he examines. I did not remember them with quite the love and appreciation he expresses. Pierce, in my recollection, was almost impenetrable and Emerson convoluted. James was idiosyncratic and Dewey, while solid and insightful, was a less than engaging writer.

Jeff's enthusiasm and clarity about the pragmatist tradition is meant to encourage you, as it encouraged me, to explore further and question assumptions like these. Jeff also means to find in this tradition a surprising consistency and hints of meaning for the American experiment, out of which this thinking emerges.

Most people who live in the United States would be surprised to learn that there have been philosophers here at all or that there is a uniquely "American" (with apologies to our comrades in the rest of the Americas) philosophical tradition. Once they imagine such a thing, however, they would be less surprised to learn that the tradition is grounded in the priority of practice over theory and that it expresses an optimistic vision. Jeff's treatment weaves these elements into a story of "awakening," an idea that, as he uses it, owes more to Asian influences than to the "Great Awakenings" identified by historians in connection with Evangelical expansions.

In calling to our attention the ways that our American pragmatists have invited us to experience the world (including ourselves) as a unity, Jeff draws on his own framework as a teacher and practitioner of meditation. We all agree, he seems to say with delight, on a paradigm of reality in which all is one, and on a notion of awakening in which we come to this realization. He makes his case with care and persuasiveness, as well as joy. Whether you want to follow him or not, you will be glad for his company in this part of the journey.

I appreciate and empathize with Jeff's efforts to connect the practices of personal growth with those of philosophical reflection, since, like him, I have had a foot in both camps. I tend to be more focused on the other theme of this book, evolution, which neither Jeff nor the authors he explores treat in quite so satisfying a way. I will return to this idea after a few words about my own struggles to do what Jeff does so well in this volume.

I arrived at graduate school in philosophy in the early 1970's and received my Ph.D. in 1978. I taught full time for a few years, then went to law school and practiced law for about a decade. During that time, I taught philosophy at night and maintained some connections with professional philosophy. In the 90's, I left the practice of law and served as Executive Director of the American Philosophical Association, the main organization of professional philosophers in the US. Since leaving that position, I have taught philosophy, developed a counseling/coaching practice (grounded in philosophy), and conducted personal growth workshops.

Perhaps these bare bones of my professional life hints at the struggle to bring serious philosophical thinking to the processes of personal growth and to integrate the personal, intimate work of self-realization into philosophical work. Jeff and I are not alone in these aspirations. Since relinquishing the narrow frame of "analytic philosophy" that predominated when I was training, the profession of philosophy in the US has welcomed, more or less, a wide variety of practical applications and connections. In addition to contributions to critical thinking and professional ethics, philosophers have taken up forms of "philosophical counseling" and "business consulting." They have also welcomed back into the fold the tradition of pragmatism that was largely ignored in the decades after Dewey's death.

My main engagement with personal growth has been as a philosophical counselor, Gestalt therapist and conductor of the Essential Experience, an intensive personal growth workshop. While all this work is grounded in philosophical assumptions, little of the practical work draws explicitly on philosophy. Clients and participants are naturally interested in their own growth and healing, not footnotes about sources. There is an anti-intellectual thread in the "self-help" world, cautioning against being too much in one's head.Yet, there is also a thread that affirms the value of intellectual development as part of personal growth, and Jeff and I share the aspiration for greater integration of heart and mind.

I have written a bit, particularly about the workshop, and participated in conferences on philosophical counseling and transformational philosophy. While this reflects some tolerance in the profession, the main work of philosophers understandably remains focused on ideas and arguments. There is resistance on both sides to integration of mind and heart.

So, it's not easy. I can imagine that some of Jeff's students may pass on this effort toward philosophical growth, trusting in the sufficiency of meditation and intuition. I urge them to stretch in the direction he indicates, to embrace intellectual growth, even when it feels confusing and disconnected from immediate experience. Trust that it will come back together. I have so urged many of the folks I have encountered in my personal growth work. And, of course, this is the converse of the urging we have both done to those philosophers and intellectuals who really are seriously disconnected from their hearts and immediate experience.

I mentioned that Jeff invites us to see more clearly the ways that the pragmatist tradition embraces unity as the ground of experience. He also urges us to see a consistent embrace of "evolution" as central to the tradition. In part, this concerns coming to terms with the emergence of Darwin's account of natural selection and its meaning for human life. It has been a challenge for every philosophical tradition to sort out what this scientific account of the emergence and development of living systems means for human nature, for religious traditions, and for public policy. The pragmatist tradition, grounded in science and the natural world, engaged this challenge with vigor and insight.

"Evolution," however, is sometimes conceived more loosely, as a synonym for growth or development. To speak of the evolution of individuals, or, on the other hand, the evolution of the universe is, I think, to use the term in this looser way. I am happier to encourage growth and development than to, as I see it, confuse things by speaking of personal evolution. Moreover, the suggestion that the universe "evolves" invites other confusions, or at least serious questions.

Perhaps there are ways to tie the strict and narrow uses of the term into a coherent whole. It seems to me that the pragmatists, and Jeff, in his account of them, gesture in this direction. While I am inclined to think that more is gained by making a sharp distinction, clarifying the scientific account and recognizing the variety of forms of growth, I appreciate the challenge of a unified account.

Jeff writes with clarity and accessibility about authors who were themselves not always easy to follow. He presents some of the ideas of Emerson, Peirce, James and Dewey with care and accuracy, as well as enthusiasm. Whether readers are coming from the philosophical tradition or the personal growth tradition, or, if like Jeff and me, they are seeking some integration, they will find in this text much to think about and feel about. And they will appreciate Jeff's consistent presence as an amiable companion.

Eric Hoffman, Ph.D.
Saint Joseph's University
Essential Experience Workshop

I wrote this book because I fell in love with American philosophy and I hope you will too.

I want you to experience the rich and dynamic vision of reality that exists in the American philosophical tradition. This is not a complete account of American philosophy by any stretch. The journey you will take through these pages is very selective, charting a specific course through a vast body of work.

What you will discover is that, for the past 200 years, some intrepid American philosophers have been exploring a vision of the universe as an overwhelmingly unified, utterly undivided and passionately indivisible evolving event. This stands in stark contrast to a universe that is more typically described as a vast expanse of infinite empty space filled with separate things.

You will see that the job of describing a fully holistic evolutionary process is supremely challenging, and requires fundamental shifts in the way we think and perceive. Please enjoy the adventure.

CHAPTER ONE

The Unity of Mind and Matter

Sit back and relax. Read and enjoy. You are about to go on an adventure of ideas. What you will discover is that there is a secret tradition of spiritual awakening obscured behind the academic façade of classical American philosophy. Many of us, especially Americans, have never been properly introduced to this profound body of work. We've run into it perhaps from time to time in bits and pieces, but no one ever sat down with us to lovingly share the intellectual riches to be found in the writings of Ralph Waldo Emerson, Charles Sanders Peirce, William James or John Dewey.

This book is not offering a complete rendering of the tradition. It will be a selective voyage designed to introduce you to what I see as a profound enlightenment tradition that was birthed and nurtured in a uniquely American fashion, and then disguised as nothing more than an academic discipline.

We will begin our story with an intellectual call to arms, or what Oliver Wendel Holmes described as an "intellectual Declaration of Independence"; although the story of the American awakening we are telling was a year old by then. Still, the date August 31, 1837 is a good date for us to start with because, on that date, Ralph Waldo Emerson delivered the commencement address to the Phi Beta Kappa Society at Harvard. The American Revolution had ended scarcely six decades earlier when Emerson stepped up to the podium and demanded an intellectual, cultural and spiritual revolution that would match the original political one.

"Perhaps the time is already come" he explained in his famous *American Scholar Address*, "when the sluggard intellect of this continent will look from under its iron lids and fill the postponed expectation of the world with something better than the exertions of mechanical skill."

The address that afternoon was advancing an inner revolution that Emerson had ignited the year before with the publication of a slim volume called *Nature*. That rather brief and innocent enough looking book had managed to set off a powder keg of intellectual and spiritual debate in and around Boston. In his book, and then again in his commencement address, Emerson was calling people to give up any secondhand understanding of reality and embrace a bold and original relationship to life. In *Nature* he writes,

> *The foregoing generations beheld God and nature face to face; we, through their eyes. Why should not we also enjoy an original relation to the universe? Why should not we have a poetry and philosophy of insight and not of tradition, and a religion by revelation to us, and not the history of theirs?*

During his entire lifetime, Emerson continually called his circle of transcendentalists to embrace his principle of Self-Reliance. By learning to connect with our higher nature, our lives become reflections of higher potentials. Counted among Emerson's associates are some of the greatest and most original thinkers of the time, and his influence did not stop with his own generation.

Not long after Emerson's death, a group of original young thinkers, three of whom were children of Emerson's closest associates, developed the philosophy of pragmatism — America's greatest contribution to world philosophy. The central message of pragmatism is that the validity of an idea lies in the practical difference it makes when put into action. The American philosopher and psychologist William James put it bluntly when he said:

> *What difference would it practically make to anyone if this notion rather than that notion were true? If no practical difference whatever can be traced, then the alternatives mean practically the same thing, and all dispute is idle. Whenever a dispute is serious, we ought to be able to show some practical difference that must follow from one side or the other's being right.*

Pragmatism flourished globally during the early decades of the 20th century. Unfortunately, on its surface it appears only to be an expression of a utilitarian sentiment that states that the truth is whatever works. This crass interpretation makes pragmatism easy to dismiss, but if we look below the surface, we find a profound philosophy of unity that rests on an insistence that mind and matter cannot exist independent of each other. Pragmatism is not an assertion of the value of utility, it is an insistence that mind and matter are not separate. Therefore, the ideas inside our heads can only be as true as they look outside in the world.

The unity of mind and matter was a foundational element in the thinking of Ralph Waldo Emerson and his band of transcendentalists. In the next generation, it would become a core conviction of William James, Charles Sanders Peirce and John Dewey, who together, developed the philosophy of pragmatism. The story I want to tell is the story about how the conviction that *mind and matter are one* blossomed into a uniquely American tradition of spiritual philosophy. We will begin our journey by exploring the assertion that mind and matter are inseparable aspects of an ultimately indivisible whole.

Mind cannot exist without matter, and matter cannot exist without mind is an essential theme that runs through the voyage of American philosophy that we will delve into in this book. Every element of mind must have a correlate in matter and all of matter must have its parallel in mind. *All insides must have an outside and all outsides must have an inside* is the holistic assumption at the heart of the American philosophy we will explore. As we will see, this foundational insistence on total unity between the inner and the outer compels a profound collective attempt to construct a new vision of reality.

"Nature is the opposite of the soul, answering to it part for part. One is seal, and one is print." said Ralph Waldo Emerson, in the *American Scholar Address.* His assertion insists that there is a necessary unity between mind and matter. Mind and matter are like two sides of a single coin. A coin is not made up of two parts that can be separated, like a hammer is made of a wooden handle and a metal head.

You cannot separate one side of a coin from the other. Even if you were to slice the coin through its edge into two halves and throw one half away, the remaining half would still have two sides. You could split the coin again and again, each time throwing away one half, and every time the half remaining would still have two sides. You cannot separate the two sides of a coin. In a similar way, some American philosophers attempted to build an understanding of reality based on the assumption that mind and matter cannot be separated, and that they have evolved as a necessary unity from the beginning of time.

The journey of discovery that you are invited to in this book is a journey into a strange and wonderful universe where everything is created from everything else. There is no inside to this universe and no outside either. There are no gaps and no lines of division. There is simply one continuous flow of reality. We, ourselves, are not a thing clinging to the surface of a planet that is, itself, floating in empty space. We are an inseparable part of an indivisible flow of reality. There is nothing that separates us from anything else and therefore we are everything there is. This is the strange and wonderful vision of the universe that was worked on during the span of about a century by two generations of American philosophers.

When I speak to people — including Americans — about American philosophy, people often look back at me somewhat bewildered. Americans are not known for their philosophy. And yet the truth is that we do have one, and it contains a magnificent vision of a universe that grows as one dynamically interconnected whole. We are not separate from the universe any more than our mouths are separate from our faces. We grew out of the universe like a leaf grows out of a tree.

This book presents an awe-inspiring vision of reality that was initiated by Ralph Waldo Emerson and later expanded upon in the philosophy of pragmatism. As you read, you will discover a new way of thinking about reality, not as a collection of interconnected parts, but as single living event that has grown - from the inside and out — since before time.

CHAPTER TWO

Evolutionary Spirituality in America

My reading of American classical philosophy reveals a tradition of unity, oneness and non-duality. It is a vision of reality which refuses to accept division, boundary and separation. Instead, it strives to see reality as a continuous whole event and works tirelessly to explain how that is possible

The term non-duality is borrowed from Eastern spiritual traditions where it literally means "not two" and points to the ultimate unity of all things. Great realizers of both the East and the West have often described experiences of deep mystical union that have left them certain that the ultimate nature of reality is oneness, or non-duality. The world of separate objects, of isolated things, is often seen in this light as a superficial illusion, that masks the deeper reality that all is one. I spent my entire adult life exploring, pursuing and studying non-dual spiritual traditions, and so I was ecstatic to find what I see as a rich and profound non-dual tradition in the classical philosophy of America.

In the development of mystical and philosophical thought in America, the experience of unity, oneness or non-duality has played a central role. A non-dual experience, when it occurs in an individual, almost invariably becomes the defining moment of an entire life. The experience of non-duality has been the prime motivator of many of the greatest realizers from traditions the world over, and yet the way that experience is interpreted varies dramatically from individual to individual, and from one tradition to the next. In the story of American philosophy, the non-dual experiences of some of America's most important thinkers have been the anchor of their life's work, and these profound experiences have been interpreted quite differently by different individuals.

And yet, in the end, I find that a selective reading of American philosophy reveals an original and authentic non-dual teaching and spiritual path.

We start our exploration with the figure of Ralph Waldo Emerson who was one of the great mystical figures in American history. He began his adult life as a minister but left the church after a fairly short time to become the most celebrated figure in the 19th century spiritual movement known as transcendentalism. Emerson enjoyed a long life as an influential essayist and speaker, and he influenced some of the greatest minds that his era produced. Henry David Thoreau, Nathaniel Hawthorne, Margaret Fuller, Walt Whitman, Emily Dickinson, Louisa May Alcott, Edgar Allan Poe, Mark Twain and many other cultural icons were shaped in part by, and either in agreement or disagreement with, Emerson and his work. The influence of Emerson on the American mind cannot be overestimated. As the contemporary literary critic Harold Bloom put it, "The mind of Emerson is the mind of America."

To understand Emerson's thinking, we must consider the nature of his deepest spiritual awakenings to non-dual oneness. In a journal entry that he wrote on April 11, 1834, he writes:

"I saw only the noble earth on which I was born, with the great Star which warms and enlightens it. I saw the clouds that hang their significant drapery over us. It was Day— that was all Heaven said."

This short quotation was taken from a larger journal entry in which Emerson described an experience of oneness with nature that he had one afternoon while walking through the Mount Auburn Cemetery in Cambridge, Massachusetts. One thing we see right away is that Emerson's experience is wedded to the wonder of the natural world. But his experience is not only an awakening to the beauty of nature as it exists around him, his realization in that moment ultimately revealed that all the seeming diversity of nature is part of one holy expression of a single creation. Heaven only said one thing. And perhaps, most importantly, he goes on in that passage to admit that he himself was as much a part of that whole as anything else. This recognition of the unified whole behind all of the apparent diversity of the world is widely considered to be the moment of enlightenment that defined Emerson's entire life.

As I picture Emerson on that day, I imagine him transfixed in a recognition of the explosion of life that he saw all around him. Emerson saw that the beauty of the plants, trees, and sky were not separate from the deep emotionally uplifting surge of exuberance that burst inside his own heart and mind in spontaneous response to seeing the beauty around him. He was as much a part of that day as anything else. There was only one thing happening — and it was day! Emerson's life's work rests on the recognition that the deepest part of human nature is completely inseparable from the rest of nature. Nature is not something that exists outside of us. We are a part of nature.

Emerson's first book was called *Nature* and it was published in 1836. The first chapter of that book includes Emerson's most often quoted description of non-dual awakening:

> *In the woods, we return to reason and faith. There I feel that nothing can befall me in life, — no disgrace, no calamity... which nature cannot repair. Standing on the bare ground, — my head bathed by the blithe air, and uplifted into infinite space, — all mean egotism vanishes. I become a transparent eyeball; I am nothing; I see all; the currents of the Universal Being circulate through me; I am part or particle of God.*

This is a beautiful and unmistakable description of the disappearance of the separate sense of self. Emerson's "transparent eyeball" metaphorically communicates the experience of pure awareness after the sense of being a separate individual has disappeared from consciousness. In this experience, you completely lose track of yourself. It is simply the experience of awareness being aware, and no sense of anyone behind it that is aware. Inherent in the experience is the undeniable recognition that one is seeing the truth — that no separate self exists in reality. This realization of "no-self" is often associated with Eastern thought, particularly the enlightenment experiences of Buddhism. In the midst of a no-self episode, it feels as if you have disappeared and yet awareness remains. Pure awareness means awareness that is free-floating beyond any attachment to a sense of self.

In my book, *The Soul of a New Self*, I describe my own experience of this state:

It is like floating on your back in the middle of the ocean. You can only see the sky above...You can even go so far that you lose all sense of your body and mind. There is just seeing. This is often called the witness state. Who is this witness? Who is it that sees through your eyes and hears through your ears? What is the source of awareness, and where does it abide? The interruption of our self-concept does not extinguish awareness. The person who was aware is no longer there, but awareness remains. Who is aware? What is aware?

Emerson had a deep appreciation for Eastern spiritual philosophy, and he incorporated many of its most profound conceptions and implications into his own thinking. In doing so, he helped ensure that the Eastern notion of non-duality would have a shaping influence in the development of American philosophy. As we shall soon see, the perplexing question of *what is aware through us* became the central tenet behind Emerson's spiritual teaching of Self-Reliance.

In this book, we are drawing upon the idea of non-duality in the more traditional Eastern sense. But, more importantly, we are exploring the characteristically Western articulation of the oneness of a universe that evolves as a single continuous whole. More specifically, we are exploring what I see as an American non-dual tradition that draws on Eastern thought at the same time that it builds on the ideas of German idealists like, Hegel, Fichte and Schelling, and ultimately responds to Darwin's conception of evolution. What was brewing in early American philosophy was an evolutionary metaphysics that describes how absolutely everything is in a constant state of evolution. This monumental endeavour took shape over about a one-hundred-year span, beginning with the writings of Ralph Waldo Emerson, and then brought into the modern age in the philosophy of pragmatism developed initially by Charles Sanders Peirce, William James and John Dewey. In this chapter, our focus will be on Emerson's early articulation of a new and thrilling vision of a universe that evolves as one vast continuous whole.

It is impossible to mark the birth date of an idea. All ideas grow out of previous ideas, and so, there is never an unquestionably clear moment in which you can honestly say that an idea appeared where it had never existed before. Still, there are certainly some useful delineations that can be used to identify the initiating point of an idea. In the case of the American expression of a non-dual evolutionary metaphysics, Emerson's publication of a barely 100-page long book called *Nature* in 1836 is as good a place to start as any. In *Nature*, Emerson first publicly described the growth of the universe as one continuous whole. Over the next eight years, the ideas that he explored in this book matured until he published an essay by the same name, in 1844, that contained a more fully articulated vision of evolutionary spirituality.

Emerson was writing about spiritual evolution more than two decades before Charles Darwin published *On the Origin of Species* — a book that would become a central concern of the pragmatists of the next generation. Emerson was a trained Christian minister and his emerging view of evolution contradicted a great deal of what he had studied in the Bible. Despite what he increasingly saw as irrefutable evidence for the physical evolution of the Earth, Emerson found it difficult to accept the materialistic viewpoint that the idea of evolution seemed to be rooted in. By 1844, his belief in evolution seemed to have solidified, while he continued to hold fast to his spiritual understanding of existence and was ready to combine the two.

In the essay *Nature*, Emerson describes how the process of evolution unfolds when he states that nature "publishes itself in creatures, reaching from particles and spicula, through transformation on transformation to the highest symmetries, arriving at consummate results without a shock or a leap." All that is needed for this miraculous progression of form, he claims, are "the two cardinal conditions of boundless space and boundless time." Pertaining to this last point, Emerson was aware that early 19th century geologists had convincingly estimated the age of the Earth to be much older than anyone had ever imagined before. The unimaginable time span of the Earth's history led Emerson to believe that nature had been afforded ample time to do her evolutionary work. Once Emerson decided that nature had indeed had enough time to evolve, his belief in evolution was cemented and he left the official church doctrine of Creationism behind. Once again in his essay *Nature*, Emerson celebrates the vast and patient creative process of the universe.

*Now we learn what patient periods must round themselves
before the rock is formed, then before the rock is broken, and
the first lichen race has disintegrated the thinnest external
plate into soil, and opened the door for the remote Flora,
Fauna, Ceres, and Pomona, to come in. How far off yet is the
trilobite! how far the quadruped! how inconceivably remote
is man! All duly arrive, and then race after race of men. It
is a long way from granite to the oyster; farther yet to Plato,
and the preaching of the immortality of the soul. Yet all must
come, as surely as the first atom has two sides.*

This passage demonstrates Emerson's embrace of an evolutionary
view of the universe, but more to the point of this book, he goes
on to describe the universe not as a collection of expanding parts,
but as a single indivisible thing. "...from the beginning to the end
of the universe, she has but one stuff," he writes, "Compound it
how she will, star, sand, fire, water, tree, man, it is still one stuff,
and betrays the same properties." The universe is not a collection
of separate objects. It is one unified whole that grows. This vision
of a universe that grows as a unified whole was picked up by the
next generation of American philosophers and that insight has
continued as an important thread throughout the subsequent
development of American thought.

Over the course of his life, Emerson didn't just describe the
process of evolution, he also attempted to explain how it worked.
Throughout a long and brilliant career, he developed a theory about
how evolution actually happens. Many of his fundamental ideas
about the evolution of the universe find themselves recast and
developed in the later works of Charles Sanders Peirce, William
James, John Dewey, and other more contemporary American
philosophers.

Included in Emerson's understanding of evolution is a sentiment
that readers of the popular 20th century thinker Ken Wilber will
recognize. In one sentence, Emerson describes evolution by saying,
"She (nature) keeps her laws, and seems to transcend them." This
combination of retention of essential elements of what is, while
simultaneously leaping into it what is next, is the foundational
formula for growth that Wilber would later capture in the phrase,
"transcend and include". In other words, evolution does not reject
its past, it expands on it by growing into new possibilities.

Emerson is not silent on the origins of the universe either. He claims that the universe begins with an "aboriginal push"; an idea that anticipates the modern Big Bang theory by nearly a century. Once this push occurs, it "propagates itself through all the balls of the system, and through every atom of every ball, through all the races of creatures, and through the history and performances of every individual."

In his evolutionary thinking, Emerson asserts that increasing the capacity for higher and higher experiences of consciousness is the inevitable and unavoidable direction of the evolutionary process, and yet he also sees that with evolutionary progress also comes evolutionary challenges. He describes the cosmic ladder of development as a "system in transition" and he implies that although evolution generally moves toward expanded consciousness, the freedom of growth also introduces aberrations and potentially dangerous deviations. As he describes it, "... men, though young, having tasted the first drop from the cup of thought, are already dissipated: the maples and ferns are still uncorrupted; yet no doubt, when they come to consciousness, they too will curse and swear." Emerson sees the challenges that self-awareness brings, and he imagines that other species will evolve to similar consciousness and face their own challenges.

In an uncharacteristically pessimistic insight, the generally optimistic Emerson admits that self-consciousness brings with it an unavoidable corruption of the perfection of nature because it gives the species that processes it the capacity to separate itself from its own source. Healing the split that self-awareness cleaves between the soul of the universe and the human self-image becomes the central focus of Emerson's mature spiritual teaching. Emerson's evolutionary theory is fundamentally a spiritual prescription for healing the split between the individual self and the soul of humanity, between the small "s" self and the big "S" Self. This healing leads, ultimately and inevitably, to the emergence of a higher consciousness in which a perfect union between the individual being and the wisdom and love of the universe is attained. Evolution, in Emerson's view, advances through a process that involves splintering off pieces of the whole and then reuniting with them. The current state of humanity is in a splintered form and will inevitably reunite with the whole of creation.

Perhaps the most surprising and progressive aspect of Emerson's evolutionary view is that it did not privilege the human experience. Although he saw consciousness as the inevitable product of evolution, he did not separate human beings from the natural process of universal growth, nor did he assume that consciousness was exclusively a human attribute. Just over twenty years after Emerson published his book called *Nature*, Charles Darwin rocked the world with a theory that gave evidence for the fact that human beings were just one more step along the ladder of evolution. Darwin's theory of natural selection explained the development of humanity by natural causes needing no supernatural intervention. Emerson's theory of spiritual evolution similarly recognized no special distinction between humanity and the rest of the natural world.

In the essay *Nature* he claims, "We talk of deviations from natural life, as if artificial life were not also natural." According to Emerson, there can be nothing unnatural in the natural process of universal growth. The creations of human beings are just as much a part of the natural evolutionary unfolding as the growth of a flower or a tree. In his own words, Emerson claims that "we need not be superstitious about towns, as if that terrific or beneficial force did not find us there also, and fashion cities. Nature who made the mason, made the house." Whatever it is that is guiding the process of evolution is not in any way separate from the will and intelligence that human beings utilize when we create. What we see is that Emerson was developing a comprehensive theory of conscious evolution long before 20th century evolutionary spiritual pioneers such as Sri Aurobindo, Pierre Teilhard de Chardin and Rudolf Steiner.

Generally speaking, Emerson's optimism about the ultimate role that humanity could play in the natural order of things seemed to know no bounds. Although he admitted that the human race is currently far from reaching its ultimate majesty and perfection, he firmly states that we will overcome our dullness and selfishness, and when that happens "...nature will look up to us." Emerson believed that humankind, in its ultimately perfected state, would be a shining achievement of the natural process of evolution and not a sullied by-product. In considering Emerson's view of the glorious potential of human growth, it is important to remember that in spite of the prominent place that Emerson held for a perfected humanity in the process of evolution, he did not see human beings as separate from that process. Any glory that humanity could attain would belong to the universe as a whole, not to us.

The imaginative leap that Emerson began to express in his writing and teaching could be described as evolutionary non-duality. As we have already stated, non-duality means oneness, or more literally not-two. Emerson is envisioning a universal evolutionary process that unfolds as a continuous whole. He does not draw a line of separation between the process of evolution and the fruits of evolution - including human beings or the fruits of human efforts.

The universe evolves through its own creations. Each new form that emerges through the process of evolution becomes the platform and the process of evolution's continued unfolding. All of the results of evolution immediately become the means for further evolution. The human species, for instance, was produced by the process of evolution and, in turn, will serve the process of evolution's continued advancement. We are both the created and the creator; the discoverer and the originator of the things we discover, because as Emerson writes, "the craft with which the world is made, runs also into the mind and character of men." In short, we are nothing less than the evolutionary process in action. As we shall see, this self-transforming view of evolution will be very strongly reflected in the later evolutionary and educational philosophies of John Dewey, but that won't happen for many decades and will be described much later in this book.

There is a holographic sensibility to Emerson's evolutionary thinking because the whole is always reflected in its entirety in all of its parts. Emerson refers to a universal intelligence that guides the process of evolution, but this universal intelligence is not separate from human intelligence. In one passage, he refers to this higher intelligence as a common sense and writes, "The common sense of Franklin, Dalton, Davy, and Black, (all great thinkers) is the same common sense which made the arrangements which now it discovers." In other words, the genius that human beings discover in nature is the same genius with which we make those discoveries. We discover ourselves in nature because we are nature. These passages demonstrate Emerson's radical deviation from church doctrine. The creator is not a god that exists separate from us. The creator is the process that created us, and we ourselves are the continuation and extension of that creative work.

Emerson's radical recognition of the divine truth of human nature began to emerge with the 1836 publication of the book *Nature*, but it was amplified tenfold with his *Divinity School Address* delivered at Harvard on July 15, 1838. If his *American Scholar Address* of 1837 was an intellectual declaration of independence, then the *Divinity School Address* was surely a declaration of independence for the human soul. Not long ago, I visited the Harvard Divinity School in Cambridge, Massachusetts, and stood behind the podium in the small lecture hall where the *Divinity School Address* had been delivered. I felt the revolutionary spirit reverberating through the dark paneled walls of the room. And I could almost feel the shock in some members of the audience as Emerson asserted that human beings were divine beings and openly criticized the church for not recognizing this. His strong rebuttal of church doctrine, in one of their own stronghold institutions, and to a group of newly trained ministers no less, was more than enough to catalyze a spiritual explosion.

One of the most grievous sins that Emerson made in his address was his assertion that Jesus was not especially blessed, but rather he was the greatest example (so far) of what all human beings could and should aspire to become. In his own words:

> *Jesus Christ belonged to the true race of prophets. He saw with open eye the mystery of the soul. Drawn by its severe harmony, ravished with its beauty, he lived in it, and had his being there. Alone in all history, he estimated the greatness of man. One man was true to what is in you and me. He saw that God incarnates himself in man, and evermore goes forth anew to take possession of his world.*

Emerson accused the church of two errors; the first was elevating the figure of Jesus Christ to a station above the rest of humanity creating a cult of personality around him.

> *Historical Christianity has fallen into the error that corrupts all attempts to communicate religion. As it appears to us, and*

as it has appeared for ages, it is not the doctrine of the soul,
but an exaggeration of the personal, the positive, the ritual.
It has dwelt, it dwells, with noxious exaggeration about the
person of Jesus.

By elevating Jesus to such an unattainable stature, the church
buries divinity in history and fails to recognize that true spiritual
emancipation is available to all of us here and now.

"Men have come to speak of the revelation as somewhat long
ago given and done, as if God were dead. The injury to faith
throttles the preacher; and the goodliest of institutions becomes
an uncertain and inarticulate voice."

Just reading the *Divinity School Address*, even in our progressive
age, can be an uncomfortable experience. I must admit that I feel
some trepidation publishing these thoughts even though I hide
safely nestled behind Emerson's podium.

Emerson recognizes that the second error of the church was an
inevitable consequence of the first. The preachers that stand
in front of the pulpits on Sundays are largely uninspired by
authentic spiritual experience and teach the gospel mainly from
an intellectual understanding and not from living revelation.
Because of this, they are unable to provoke a genuine experience
of the divine in the hearts of others.

> *The spirit only can teach. Not any profane man, not any*
> *sensual, not any liar, not any slave can teach, but only he can*
> *give, who has; he only can create, who is. The man on whom*
> *the soul descends, through whom the soul speaks, alone can*
> *teach. Courage, piety, love, wisdom, can teach; and every man*
> *can open his door to these angels, and they shall bring him*
> *the gift of tongues. But the man who aims to speak as books*
> *enable, as synods use, as the fashion guides, and as interest*
> *commands, babbles. Let him hush.*

Emerson felt it was his duty to encourage a new generation to strike
out on their own and find an authentic path to the immediacy of
truth. Scripture, as wise as it may be, can only tell us how truth
was revealed to others in the past. Emerson started a spiritual
revolution by calling us to look towards nature to find spirit as
it exists today.

Yourself a new-born bard of the Holy Ghost, — cast behind you all conformity, and acquaint men at first hand with Deity. Look to it first and only, that fashion, custom, authority, pleasure, and money, are nothing to you, — are not bandages over your eyes, that you cannot see, — but live with the privilege of the immeasurable mind.

Perhaps Emerson should have anticipated the enormous backlash his address would ignite, yet he never quite seemed to understand how he had managed to cause such a tremendous public retaliatory reaction. The *Divinity School Address*, and the controversy surrounding it, propelled Emerson onto a trajectory that would make him an international superstar of the spirit. He had effectively become the voice that would define the alternative spiritual movement in America.

CHAPTER THREE

Surrendering to Evolution

If we look at the last chapter, we will find three elements that we can use to characterize the theory of evolutionary spirituality that Emerson introduced into the American mind over the course of his lifetime.

The first element of Emerson's evolutionary spirituality is his profound awakening to unity, oneness, and non-duality. Emerson realized that the universe and everything in it, including human beings, was one continuous whole event. The second element was his embrace of the process of evolution, and his understanding that this process was an expression of the creative force of nature and the universe. The third element that characterizes his evolutionary spirituality is his recognition that true human maturation means growing into our own unique expression of divinity. From these three elements, Emerson created an evolutionary view of spiritual growth in which the universe evolved to produce human beings who were then destined to participate in their own further evolution toward a divine destiny.

Emerson ended his essay *Nature* by asking, "What is the end sought?" He quickly answers his own question by saying, "Plainly to secure the ends of good sense and beauty, from the intrusion of deformity or vulgarity of any kind." The universe, in short, is ultimately good. Emerson has a truly optimistic view of progress and evolution, yet he must contend with the facts: If the universe is an evolutionary process that is heading toward its own most highly perfected form, then what necessitates all the suffering and corruption in the world? Why does humanity find itself in such a seemingly undeveloped state in so many ways?

Emerson has an answer. He believes that humankind has lost its evolutionary way. "Thought, virtue, beauty, were the ends;" he claims:

> (...) but it was known that men of thought and virtue sometimes had the headache, or wet feet, or could lose good time whilst the room was getting warm in winter days. Unluckily, in the exertions necessary to remove these inconveniences, the main attention has been diverted to this object; the old aims have been lost sight of, and to remove friction has come to be the end.

We lost our way on the evolutionary journey to our own divinity by temporarily becoming preoccupied with the quest for creature comforts. It was necessary that we create ease in life so that we would have the time and space necessary to engage in our own evolution, but we have become side-tracked, lost in the never-ending quest for greater security and luxury. Emerson parodies this state of affairs by describing humanity as "one who has interrupted the conversation of a company to make his speech, and now has forgotten what he went to say." This misguided state of human affairs has resulted in "an aimless society, of aimless nations."

What is the solution? How can humanity reclaim its evolutionary pathway to higher consciousness? First, "We cannot bandy words with nature, or deal with her as we deal with persons. If we measure our individual forces against hers, we may easily feel as if we were the sport of an insuperable destiny." Nature is simply too powerful and too awesome for us to control or guide.

> But if, instead of identifying ourselves with the work, we feel that the soul of the workman streams through us, we shall find the peace of the morning dwelling first in our hearts, and the fathomless powers of gravity and chemistry, and, over them, of life, pre-existing within us in their highest form.

Evolution is not something that we can do, but we can surrender ourselves to the evolutionary process and allow it to work through us. If we see ourselves as agents of a vast evolutionary process, then the power and intelligence of that universal process "streams through us."

Emerson sees a divinely unfolding evolutionary process that runs unendingly forward from divinity to divinity. Starting with the mind of God, traveling through the chain of nature's creations and finding its way to the mind of humankind.

> *The divine circulations never rest nor linger. Nature is the incarnation of a thought, and turns to a thought again, as ice becomes water and gas. The world is mind precipitated, and the volatile essence is forever escaping again into the state of free thought.*

So far, we have explored Emerson's early thinking. Now we must turn to the more mature thought of his later years. In 1860, he published an essay called *Fate* in a collection called The Conduct of Life. This essay is written by an older Emerson, one who has worked and taught for nearly 3 decades and who has found some of his youthful — perhaps naïve — optimism tempered by time. In his earlier evolutionary philosophy, Emerson eagerly described how nature would inevitably climb up through the ladder of animal species to the final perfected state of humankind. In those earlier works, he recognized that the human species had lost its way — how we became distracted by the pursuit of material comforts — but he still believed that all we needed to do was remember and reclaim our original cosmic motive for being and restart our ascent up the evolutionary ladder.

In *Fate*, the aging sage feels compelled to introduce a more somber force that he now realizes acts to counter the upward march toward nature's perfection. It is the force of Fate, which he refers to as the laws of the world. In using the word Fate, Emerson is not referring to things that are destined to be, he is more generally referring to the tendency of things to resist change and continue on as they have been. The forces of Fate act to limit us. They are the negating forces to the creative power of nature and the influence of human will. Emerson describes his discovery of these opposing forces by saying, "Once we thought, positive power was all. Now we learn, that negative power, or circumstance, is half."

The influence of Fate is found embedded in the very circumstances of life. Fate touches us through both personal and cultural circumstances, and it acts as a drag on our development and forward movement. Fate is the inherent friction of the world. It is the restraining momentum of habit and inertia. It is the existence of *fate* in nature that makes the process of evolution take so much time. Emerson confesses:

> *The book of Nature is the book of Fate. She turns the gigantic pages, — leaf after leaf, — never returning one. One leaf she lays down, a floor of granite; then a thousand ages, and a bed of slate; a thousand ages, and a measure of coal; a thousand ages, and a layer of marl and mud: vegetable forms appear; her first misshapen animals, zoophyte, trilobium, fish; then, saurians, — rude forms, in which she has only blocked her future statue, concealing under these unwieldy monsters the fine type of her coming king. The face of the planet cools and dries, the races meliorate, and man is born.*

In his earlier works, a more innocent Emerson imagined the possibility of a perfected spiritual state of human beings; a state in which the individual will was finally and completely given over to the omnipotent will of the universal soul of humanity. Over the course of time, he became discouraged because he saw how his own achievement of this perfect state eluded even his best efforts. He began to realize that a strong intention to become divinely Self-Reliant was not enough to ensure the attainment of that goal.

And yet Fate, as Emerson describes it, is not wholly separate from our own will: "Every spirit makes its house; but afterwards the house confines the spirit." We are the universal source of evolution as well as its product. It is we, as universal spirit, who had initiated the process of evolution, and it is we, as individual spirit, who must struggle toward our perfected state though the challenges of the same process that we created. We made the rules and now we must evolve by them.

Emerson wondered how it could be possible to evolve to the perfected state in the span of only one lifetime given the weight and drag that Fate places on our development? How could a man like him, born into the limiting circumstances of 19th century New England, hope to achieve mystical perfection before death separated him from this earthly existence? It seemed to him impossible that so much evolution could ever happen in the span of just one lifetime. Then Emerson realized the answer; he had encountered the solution to the dilemma of time in both the mysticism of the East and in the early Greek thought of Plato.

What made it possible for human beings to attain their perfected state was the fact that they did not live just one lifetime — we reincarnate to use the Eastern term, or, as the Greeks referred to it, our soul transmigrates. In the essay *Fate* he writes, "We rightly say of ourselves, we were born, and afterward we were born again, and many times. We have successive experiences so important, that the new forgets the old..."

The idea of reincarnation can be found in Emerson's early book *Representative Men* written in 1850, in which he states, "We are tendencies, or rather, symptoms, and none of us complete. We touch and go and sip the foam of many lives. Rotation is the law of nature." Even earlier in an essay called *History*, first published as part of a series of essays in 1841, he had already claimed that, "The philosophical perception of identity through endless mutations of form makes him know the Proteus...The transmigration of souls is no fable."

In the essay *Nominalist and Realist* published in 1844, Emerson states quite clearly:

> *Nothing is dead: men feign themselves dead, and endure mock funerals and mournful obituaries, and there they stand looking out of the window, sound and well, in some new and strange disguise. Jesus is not dead: he is very well alive: nor John, nor Paul, nor Mahomet, nor Aristotle; at times we believe we have seen them all and could easily tell the names under which they go.*

Extending Emerson's words, we see our soul in the middle of a journey of many lifetimes — traveling through the form of every living and non-living thing. Across an abundance of time, it traces a slow path of evolutionary development toward perfection. This is the image that Emerson expressed in his writing. And so, we don't have to make the whole evolutionary leap to perfection in just one lifetime. We have already been living many lifetimes and will live many more before our development is done.

In Emerson's account of evolutionary spirituality, the human soul is on a journey of its own creation — a journey from its original source through the process of manifestation to a perfected state of purity. And the soul has many lifetimes to make this journey.

"Man is ... a stupendous antagonism." Emerson exclaims. Human beings have a strength of will that can antagonize and challenge the imposed limitations of Fate with a power that comes from creation itself because within us is "the lightning which explodes and fashions planets."

This duel of power and Fate is inherent in the act of creation. As we battle against the restrictions of Fate, we "bring up our conduct to the loftiness of nature." The struggle against limitation is what teaches us courage, refines our soul and delivers us to a lofty height of purity and a direct connection to the higher power of our nature.

> I see that when souls reach a certain clearness of perception, they accept a knowledge and motive above selfishness. A breath of will blows eternally through the universe of souls in the direction of the Right and Necessary. It is the air which all intellects inhale and exhale, and it is the wind which blows the worlds into order and orbit.

As we come to this tremendous pinnacle of being, we begin to see our true nature as universal mind and "seeing its immortality, he says, I am immortal; seeing its invincibility, he says, I am strong. It is not in us, but we are in it. It is of the maker, not of what is made. All things are touched and changed by it."

We may all be on this journey to immortality, but we are not necessarily all traveling at the same pace. "Of two men, each obeying his own thought, he whose thought is deepest will be the strongest character. Always one man more than another represents the will of Divine Providence to the period." Emerson seems clear that, at any given time, there will be different degrees of awakening exhibited by different individuals. The true representatives of Divine Providence are heroes who see the way to go and take it. They are the individuals who lead humanity forward, and create the trails and the pathways that others will follow. In this way, the evolution of extraordinary individuals becomes the guiding force of evolutionary spirituality.

We have now established the contours and development of Emerson's evolutionary spirituality. The evolutionary worldview that Emerson described established a precedent and a foundation that later American philosophers would build upon.

Next, we must venture to the heart of creation. You see, for Emerson, the universe was not a static backdrop that existed out there beyond us; a stage upon which the drama of evolution unfolds. The evolving universe is an organically growing whole and, in order to find the true mechanisms of evolution, we must look within to the source of our own consciousness.

Our goal is to uncover, within the tradition of American philosophy, an authentic enlightenment tradition. A mind-expanding view on who we are and what it really means to be human. In fact, what we will discover is a tradition which sees all of reality evolving holistically as a continuous whole. Ultimately, we will find that, we ourselves, cannot be separate from the universe in which we live. We are not just an evolving being in the universe. We are the evolving universe itself.

CHAPTER FOUR

The Universal Soul

The next part of the story I want to tell begins with a discussion about two of the most profound spiritual questions we can ask, "Who are we? And how did we get here?"

One of the long-standing debates around this question involves the mental and physical aspects of our being. What came first, mind or matter? Are we intelligent matter—stuff that got smart—or are we incarnate spirit—smarts that grew stuff?

As human beings that have both physical bodies and mental experience, these questions are virtually unavoidable. We have bodies and we have consciousness—mind and matter, body and soul. Which one are we? Which came first? Which is ultimately real?

Many great religious traditions have tended toward the outlook that we are spiritual beings that became flesh. First there was God—pure spirit—and from God came us.

Our more recent scientific understanding of reality is rooted in the opposite belief, that we are matter that evolved into life and eventually became intelligent.

One of the profound, and for some troubling, implications of the view that we are forms emerging from spirit is that it places the source of our being outside of the physical universe. While our bodies exist and act here, in the world, the true source of our being is to be found in a transcendent realm outside of the world. If this is true, then the source of who we are stands outside of the laws of nature that govern the rest of the world. We are ultimately supernatural beings.

If, on the other hand, we are matter that has grown into consciousness, then our awareness is nothing more than the final end product of a series of complex material interactions. We are the natural and inevitable outgrowth of nature and her laws. Our actions and thoughts unfold organically, and are governed by the same intricate demands of cause and effect as the rest of the world. The unfolding of our lives is the inevitable result of natural forces no different than the movement of a leaf blowing in the wind is the result of the laws of energy and friction.

The distinction between these views is the difference between the philosophical positions of idealism and materialism. Idealists believe that some form of mind or consciousness is the primary source of everything in the universe, and that all material and sensual elements of reality are secondary to mind. Materialists lean in the opposite direction. They see matter as the primary reality of the universe and mind as a secondary outgrowth of material interactions.

The philosophical challenge that materialism must answer is to provide an explanation for how our subjective experience of consciousness is produced through the interactions of material elements. The challenge faced by idealism is to explain exactly what the nature of the mysterious transcendent mind is.

In 1825, the English poet and theologian Samuel Taylor Coleridge published a book called *Aids to Reflection* that helped shape the thinking of Ralph Waldo Emerson and the American transcendentalists. In what has been described as a misreading of Immanuel Kant's *Critique of Pure Reason*, Coleridge identifies two distinctly different kinds of consciousness, or ways of knowing. He refers to one of these as "understanding", which he defines as "An abstraction which the human mind forms by reflecting on its own thoughts and forms of thinking." This kind of knowing is a natural product of the process of mind and it is bound up in, and limited by, language. He also asserts that it is a process that does not requires the existence of a "self" to enact. It is not an activity performed by a person. It is a natural process of the lawful interaction of mental elements, a simple unfolding of the characteristics of the mind in nature.

Coleridge calls the other form of consciousness "reason", and describes it as a form of knowing that appears spontaneously without warning or precursor. Reason is the spontaneous knowing that does not arise through the interaction of pre-existing mental elements. It appears whole and complete before the eye of the mind. It is not an understanding constructed from, or derived through, any thought process. It is a direct and self-authenticating recognition of truth. Reason is unavoidable, and this direct knowing of truth happens spontaneously and compulsively. There is no process that leads to the knowing of reason. It just happens. We simply cannot help but know it.

At the level of reason, reality forces itself upon us immediately. Direct sense impressions — smells, tastes, sensations, sounds, and sights — simply appear in awareness. We don't call them into being, and we cannot alter or avoid the way they present themselves. They appear spontaneously without provocation and they impress themselves upon us in ways we cannot avoid. Therefore, according to Coleridge, these things surely must be real. Ideas and intuitions also — upon their initial appearance — share the same unalterable immediacy of presence and therefore must also be real.

According to Coleridge and later Emerson, the world presents itself to us through a series of spontaneous, immediate, and unalterable first impressions. At its core — before we can do anything about it — our experience appears to us as a relentless parade of pure experiences.

American transcendentalism and pragmatism both recognize the profound significance of the fact that our experience of knowing comes in two distinct forms. Coleridge spoke of these as reason and understanding, Emerson was inclined to speak about them as intuition and understanding, and later William James and the American pragmatists would refer to the same distinction as the difference between experience and understanding.

Experience is the direct knowing-of-things that present themselves to us without our doing anything. It is immediately and directly present, and so it cannot be denied. If I see a ghost in the attic, I can deny that it is a ghost — but I cannot reasonably deny that I saw something that seemed like seeing a ghost. We can deny our interpretation of our experience — our understanding of it — but we cannot deny the fact of having it.

Understanding is the knowing-about-things derived from the language of thought. It is secondary, and subject to error and revision. Understanding-about-things is important, but it is the immediately experienced knowing of reason that Coleridge and Emerson saw as the true source of our being. And both of them saw reason as the source of the human soul.

This is where we pick up our story again because Emerson, following Coleridge's lead, envisions a universal human soul that is shared by all. The universal nature of soul is what enables Emerson to imagine that the universe is one continuous unfolding event.

The modern understanding of soul tends to be personal. We imagine that each human being has one and that the soul is a phantom-like inner being that contains our conscience and moral fiber. For Coleridge and Emerson, the soul was not something exclusively held by any single individual. It was a living dimension of the universe from which all life flowed. This vision of the soul was so powerful that it ignited the imaginations of the American transcendentalists and influenced the later development of American pragmatism.

"LIFE is the one universal soul," Coleridge writes, "which, by virtue of the enlivening Breath, and the informing Word, all organized bodies have in common, each after its kind."

According to Coleridge, all beings are enlivened by the same universal soul: a field of pure knowing that all human beings exist within and which is the true source of our awareness.

When Ralph Waldo Emerson later wrote, "I become a transparent eye-ball; I am nothing; I see all; the currents of the Universal Being circulate through me; I am part or particle of God," he was evoking Coleridge's notion of the human soul. In other places, Emerson spoke of the soul as "the background of our being" and as the "light (that) shines through us upon things."

The soul is pure knowing before anything is known. It is pure subjectivity with no object yet to witness. The metaphor that Coleridge and Emerson employed to capture the nature of the soul was light.

Consider that if you shine a flashlight into space, you see nothing. The light shines out from the flashlight but won't return to strike your eye unless it reflects off of the surface of something else. So, imagine a field of pure light emanating from within you spreading out in all directions. Without an object to reflect off of, the light simply continues to spread outward into the emptiness; but when an object appears, the light reflects back for us to see it. That is why the process of thinking and contemplating was spoken of as reflection.

Human beings do not have reason as much as we live in a field of reason; an ocean of light. We are surrounded by infinite potential for knowing but know nothing until something appears to be known. Once an object appears in the emptiness, we know it immediately. The potential for seeing has been there all along and the transparent eyeball was always waiting in anticipation, but all remains in darkness until something appears to be known.

According to Coleridge and Emerson, the human soul, or reason, is not something that we possess. It is a field of pure knowing that underlies all of reality. This is an idealistic position because it says that we live in a universe that is most fundamentally composed of pure universal intelligence.

Many of us have been taught that the source of our consciousness is within us. We assume that knowing is something that happens inside of us, and that your knowing occurs inside of you. Coleridge and Emerson were working with a very different assumption. Rather than something that happens inside of us, knowing is something that happens in the universe that we live in. We may experience knowing inside of us, but the knowing that we are experiencing is coming from a universal field of awareness that exists all around and through us. In his writings and teachings, Emerson used the term the Over-Soul to capture the essence of this foundational consciousness that is the source of all human awareness. In his essay called *The Over-Soul*, Emerson writes:

> *We live in succession, in division, in parts, in particles. Meantime within man is the soul of the whole; the wise silence; the universal beauty, to which every part and particle is equally related; the eternal ONE. And this deep power in which we exist, and whose beatitude is all accessible to us, is not only*

self-sufficing and perfect in every hour, but the act of seeing and the thing seen, the seer and the spectacle, the subject and the object, are one. We see the world piece by piece, as the sun, the moon, the animal, the tree; but the whole, of which these are the shining parts, is the soul.

Emerson became known as the sage of Concord, Massachusetts, and he would teach a doctrine of what he called Self-Reliance to anyone who came to see him. His notion of Self-Reliance had nothing to do with the rugged individualism that it is sometimes confused with because the Self that he wanted us to rely on was not the ego or personality. It was the big "S" Self or the Over-Soul. According to Emerson, surrendering to this deeper self is the birth of true human greatness and virtue:

What we commonly call man, the eating, drinking, planting, counting man, does not, as we know him, represent himself, but misrepresents himself. Him we do not respect, but the soul, whose organ he is, would he let it appear through his action, would make our knees bend. When it breathes through his intellect, it is genius; when it breathes through his will, it is virtue; when it flows through his affection, it is love.

And Emerson does not at all see the soul as a merely passive source of human knowledge. The Over-Soul is a forward-moving, creative, and ultimately world-building force:

The soul looketh steadily forwards, creating a world before her, leaving worlds behind her... The soul's advances are not made by gradation, such as can be represented by motion in a straight line; but rather by ascension of state, such as can be represented by metamorphosis, — from the egg to the worm, from the worm to the fly.

The soul is the field of pure knowing at the foundation of human consciousness, and the source of all of reality. And this pure knowing is evolving. The separate things in the universe are not evolving. Rather, it is the imaginative power of the one universal mind that is expanding and growing with each new form that it envisions into being.

The next generation of American philosophers did not have the same strong religious ties that both Coleridge and Emerson had.

They were born into a rapidly modernizing age and were more influenced by the rising tide of science. In the next few chapters, we will explore how Charles Sanders Peirce and William James both developed conceptions of reality with striking similarities to Emerson's vision of the human soul. Peirce and James built upon the notion of an underlying field of consciousness, while simultaneously moving away from a religious context and toward a scientific one. In the next chapter, we will look at the evolutionary philosophy that was developed by Charles Sanders Peirce.

CHAPTER FIVE

A Co-Emerging Universe

Ralph Waldo Emerson was the central figure surrounding the transcendentalist circle of Concord, Massachusetts. This circle included some of the greatest minds of the time, and one of those was a famous mathematician named Benjamin Peirce. Our story continues with Benjamin Peirce's son, Charles Sanders, who would become equally well known for his erratic temperament and his unparalleled genius.

The two chapters that I have dedicated to the evolutionary philosophy of Charles Sanders Peirce will likely be the most difficult in the book. As you shall soon learn, Peirce was an extraordinarily free thinker. His thinking was deep in the sense that he questioned even the most fundamental assumptions about the nature of existence, and his conclusions challenge the limits of our imagination. For this reason, I have chosen to spend one chapter guiding you through one avenue of Peirce's thought process, and then will take you back up through this unusual body of work from another angle. In this way, I hope to give you the most comprehensive understanding of his work in a limited amount of space.

Charles Sanders Peirce was Benjamin Peirce's second born son, and he was undoubtedly a towering genius. He wrote extensively for numerous philosophical journals and influenced the ideas of many of the greatest thinkers of his time. He was a brilliant scientist who made important contributions to various fields; he was one of the originators of the discipline of semiotics and a pioneer of the theory of language. During his life, Peirce would become the lifelong friend of another great American philosopher, William James, whose father was also a close friend of Emerson's. Together,

Peirce and James would invent the philosophy of pragmatism and set a course for American philosophy that continues to this day.

In spite of his genius and his many important discoveries, Peirce's work remained relatively unknown outside of professional philosophical circles until it was unearthed decades after his death. He never managed to complete a comprehensive book of his ideas, and a great deal of his writing exists only in fragments and incomplete drafts. He only ever taught for one university, Johns Hopkins, and for only one semester. In fact, Peirce's only consistent employment was with the United States Coast Survey and the only reason he was able to hold that job was due to the influence of his famous father. Shortly after Benjamin Peirce died, his son lost his position with the US Coast Survey and, in the end, Peirce would die an obscure figure living penniless in Milford, Pennsylvania. If it had not been for the support and the charity of his friend William James, Peirce's work might have remained completely undiscovered, but luckily it exists for us to study and contemplate today.

Charles Sanders Peirce believed that the entire universe was evolving. And he really meant the entire universe and absolutely everything in it. Even the seemingly immutable laws of time, space, and physics, he believed, had all evolved as part of one continuous whole event. Peirce was obsessed with understanding the nature of an evolving universe and spent his entire life trying to develop a theory of evolution that could account for the emergence of absolutely everything — including the existence of time, space, causality and natural laws. He had read about Darwin's theory of evolution but he saw that Darwin took the existence of things like time and space for granted, and he didn't want to take anything for granted. He wanted to know how a universe could evolve from before time and space to now — from nothing to all that currently exists.

Most of us believe in evolution, but when we think about it, we tend to imagine species that evolve inside a universe that was already here when the process of evolution began. Peirce believed that not only do the things in the universe evolve, but the universe itself evolves. Peirce took one simple observation that each of us makes every day as definitive proof that the universe is evolving: the fact that we cannot precisely predict the future. For Peirce, this was all the evidence he needed to know that our universe is evolving.

Peirce was a scientist — in fact, he was a great one — and this, in spite of the fact that his view of the universe stood in direct opposition to the materialistic and deterministic views that were more the norm of the science at the time. He didn't see a material universe governed predictably by natural laws. He saw a growing universe, a living universe, that was fundamentally conscious.

Determinism can be thought of as the belief that "nothing comes from nothing". Everything comes from some set of initial conditions, as part of a perfectly predictable chain of cause and effect, leading unwaveringly to an inevitable outcome. According to determinism, if we knew all the initial conditions and understood all the laws of cause and effect, we could accurately predict everything about the future. The reason we fail to be able to predict the future is only because we do not know all of the initial conditions and the laws that govern them well enough.

Peirce believed that our inability to accurately predict the future was not a reflection of our lack of knowledge or understanding; it was because our universe is inherently creative, constantly in a state of flux and spontaneous emergence. New things are continuously coming into being in ways that are impossible to predict. Nothing is fixed, everything is shifting and changing all the time. According to Peirce, the essence and ground of our universe is not matter. The true essence of the universe is spontaneous creation. He called the source of this constant creativity Firstness. Firstness is the potential for novelty. It creates the possibility of being first. An exploration of Peirce's conception of Firstness reveals an idea with remarkable similarities to the way Coleridge and Emerson had imagined the human soul.

What evidence did Peirce have for assuming the universe was undetermined and spontaneous? And that novelty, spontaneity, and chance must be built into its very fabric?

In his work with the US Coast Survey, Peirce was an expert in measurement, and in his scientific work, he was constantly striving to make measurements with increasingly accurate precision. He knew, from his own experience, that the universe was constantly in flux because the more precisely he managed to measure, the more impossible it was to get the exact same measurement twice. Common wisdom would tell us that this was due to the inevitable errors we make when measuring. We naturally assume that reality itself is the same, but we're not capable of measuring the same way each time.

Peirce was not a common thinker and he realized that we were just assuming that the universe wasn't changing. When two measurements of the same thing came out differently, Peirce didn't assume he had made a mistake; he assumed he was witnessing a fluctuation in reality. He believed the reason we get different results when measuring the same things more than once is due to the fact that the thing itself is changing. We are encountering the flickering nature of reality. The universe is not exact, it has a little bit of chance and fluidity built into it. You measure something once and it is one size; you measure it again and find that it is a slightly different size. The universe has changed, shifted, moved, since the first time you measured it.

Peirce was imagining an indeterminate universe — one that was not fixed and certain. He was a century ahead of his time in anticipating the new physics of relativity and the science of quantum mechanics. And his ideas on the inexact nature of reality would serve as part of the inspiration for Werner Heisenberg's famous uncertainty principle.

The universe is not a solid and immutable stage upon which evolution takes place. The universe itself is changing all the time. Novelty, spontaneity, and chance are built into its fabric. Firstness was the term Peirce used to describe the underlying source of spontaneity in the universe.

Peirce was determined to understand the origins of an evolving universe like ours. He wanted to know what was the absolutely first thing that needed to exist to make evolution possible. Whatever emerged first in an evolving universe would evolve with the quality of being first and therefore that quality, the quality of Firstness, had to already exist. An evolving universe could only emerge if the quality of Firstness was already present.

What is the quality of being first?

One thing that comes to mind when thinking about the quality of being first is the singularity or oneness of it. There can only be one first. There is only one person that comes in first in a running race. If two people arrive at the finish line at the same time, we say they tied for first, and being tied implies being bound together into one. The most obvious element of the quality of Firstness is that *it is that which arrives before any other*.

Peirce didn't stop at only one quality though. In his essay *A Guess at the Riddle*, Peirce describes Firstness, and captures the essence of oneness, more beautifully than almost any other writing I have ever encountered on the subject:

> *The idea of the absolutely First must be entirely separated from all conception of or reference to anything else; for what involves a second is itself a second to that second. The First must therefore be present and immediate, so as not to be second to a representation. It must be fresh and new, for if old it is second to its former state. It must be initiative, original, spontaneous, and free; otherwise it is second to a determining cause. It is also something vivid and conscious; so only it avoids being the object of some sensation. It precedes all synthesis and all differentiation; it has no unity and no parts. It cannot be articulately thought, assert it, and it has already lost its characteristic innocence; for assertion always implies a denial of something else. Stop to think of it, and it has flown! What the world was to Adam on the day he opened his eyes to it, before he had drawn any distinctions, or had become conscious of his own existence—that is first, present, immediate, fresh, new, initiative, original, spontaneous, free, vivid, conscious, and evanescent. Only, remember that every description of it must be false to it.*

Firstness, we can imagine, is the field of spontaneous creative potential that everything else emerges from. It is a quivering uncertainty out of which new and novel things arise. This is the starting point of Peirce's evolutionary cosmology, but he came to understand that, in order to fully explain the evolutionary process, there had to be two other essential qualities of reality. He called these Secondness and Thirdness.

Peirce did not see a universe of vacuous empty space filled with a collection of separate but interacting material things. Instead, he saw a continuous whole universe that was composed of only three essential elements that co-emerge and co-evolve as one. Be forewarned that his vision of a trifold reality is as challenging to grasp as it is brilliant to behold.

In Peirce's vision, all of creation is built from the interplay of only three essential characteristics that combine and recombine in an infinite variety of permutations. These three essential qualities do not exist in separation — they co-emerge together — and the presence of all three at once is the minimal requirement for something to exist at all. There cannot be anything real that exists if any one or more of these three characteristics is missing. All three must be present in order for there to be any reality at all.

To better understand the co-emergent nature of these three essential qualities, imagine a piece of blank white paper. Now imagine a circle being drawn on the paper. A circle is a combination of three elements, an inside, an outside, and the curved line that separates the two. You cannot have a circle without all three of these elements present.

As you drew the circle, you started with a curved line that already had two sides to it. Once the loop of the circle was closed, one side of the line became the inside of the circle and the other side became the outside. The circle is not built out of an inside, an outside, and a boundary that can all three be separated like the bricks that build a house. As you draw the line that defines the circle, the inside and the outside of the circle co-emerge with the line from the start. Similarly, our universe arises in co-emerging triads of Firstness, Secondness, and Thirdness.

In order to get a sense of how the universe emerges, we need to understand the nature of Firstness, Secondness, and Thirdness.

Firstness we have already defined as pure novelty and spontaneity. It is the quality of being first; the ability to appear without cause or history. It is the magic spark of creation that is the essence of existence. It is the field of pure potential that creates the ground for anything to exist at all.

Secondness is what Peirce described as brute contact. It is the pure experience of coming in contact with another — a second. It has nothing to do with the qualities of the other. It is merely the experience of making contact. It is simply the recognition that another exists without knowing anything at all about the other. Secondness has no qualities other than the quality of "being in contact".

Thirdness can be thought of as relationship and understanding. It is the set of relations that make it possible for the qualities of something to be known. Thirdness is most of what we experience in the world because we experience everything as a relationship or comparison with something else. For example, I experience this as a book because it is either similar to other things that I know are books, or different from other things that I know are not books.

We could alternatively name these three qualities: existence, contact, and understanding. And in Peirce's evolutionary philosophy, everything else is constructed from combinations of these. Peirce believed that, over time, we would be able to explain all of creation as the emergence of relationships of understanding that arise out of connected essences.

We can use the art of pointillism — a style of painting in which a painter creates images using only tiny dots of colour — as a metaphor to help us picture what Peirce was getting at. From a distance, the tiny dots present a cohesive image, for example, of people, trees, and flowers. When you get close to the painting, however, you see the truth that each figure, every element of the painting, is constructed from those tiny dots of pure colour. Peirce would say that if you look closely enough at reality, you will only see combinations of existence, contact, and understanding.

To get an experiential sense of what Peirce was pointing toward, imagine reaching your hand into a paper bag. You know that something exists in the bag, but you don't know what it is. Initially your finger touches the object and you experience pure contact; Secondness. Then, the qualities of the touch begin to emerge. The object is hard, smooth and cold. These qualities you only know in relationship to other things you have touched. You are beginning to experience the Thirdness of the thing. Suddenly, you recognize that it is an apple and the object becomes a specific something that has relations to many other things that you know about. In fact, it now relates to an entire world of other objects. The world of objects, which means the world we live in, is a world of Thirdnesses, a world of relationships and understanding but, of course, Thirdness cannot exist without Secondness (contact) and Firstness (existence).

In this chapter, we began with Peirce's realization that the universe is inherently creative, constantly producing novelty that cannot be predicted or known. This capacity to create from nothing is the source of life, consciousness and evolution. We went on to explore Peirce's attempt to discover all of the essential building blocks that the universe needed in order to create the wondrous diversity that we see around us. He determined, in the end, that there were only three things necessary. He believed that what he was describing was so foundational to our experience of the world that any ordinary words he used to describe them would be limiting and ultimately misleading. He decided to call them Firstness, Secondness and Thirdness, which might be awkward, but most directly expressed his meaning. Peirce recognized that his theory was too abstract for most people to understand. In fact, he believed it would take the rest of humanity 200 years to fully develop the theory he had started to articulate.

Over the course of his lifetime, Peirce described this three-fold nature of reality in many different ways. One of those ways involved associating them with the pronouns *I*, *me* and *it*. Firstness was associated with *I*, Secondness with *me*, Thirdness with *it*. The contemporary philosopher Ken Wilber credits Peirce with having inspired his own Integral Theory in which Wilber would add a fourth category, *its*, to create his four-quadrant model of reality.

We are not yet done with Peirce. His ideas are too important for just one pass through. The most remarkable thing about Peirce was his bold and wildly inventive commitment to relentless inquiry. And so, in the next chapter, we will take another look at this great thinker, this time starting with his commitment to open-ended investigation, and then slowly circling back to the ideas of Firstness, Secondness, and Thirdness, until we end with his conception of Evolutionary Love.

CHAPTER SIX

Inquiry, Language and Evolutionary Love

One of the main themes running through this book is about how the concept of an evolving universe was embraced in the developing tradition of American philosophy. The idea of evolution had expanded the realm of possibility far beyond our imagination. We were not just living and learning; we were evolving! And we could no longer predict how much change was possible, in much the same way that a caterpillar cannot predict that it will emerge from the cocoon as a butterfly. The roof had come off and we now found ourselves with the power to guide the growth of our individual future and of life itself.

A realization this big necessitated a radical shift in consciousness. We needed to open and embrace a view of ourselves and reality that was vaster than our minds could grasp. We needed an inner awakening that was big enough to hold what we had discovered. Emerson was sharing this potential for inner awakening as early as 1836. Charles Sanders Peirce and William James picked up the ball from him and carried it into the start of the next century. From there, another great American philosopher, John Dewey, would make a long run past the midpoint of the twentieth century. But let's not get too far ahead of ourselves. We still have to take a second look at the genius of Charles Sanders Peirce.

Peirce's unconventional thinking had its roots in his semiotic thinking. Semiotics is the study of how the signs and symbols of language communicate and hold meaning. Peirce was one of the inventors of that field of study. He recognized that the human mind creates intelligibility through a never-ending succession of signs pointing to other signs, in what becomes an infinitely complex web of interrelated meaning. What makes Peirce's vision of reality profound is that he doesn't assume that signs are pointing *toward* a reality that exists without them. He sees signs as an inseparable, essential and integral *part of* reality.

In a paper called *The Architecture of Theories*, Peirce claimed that objective idealism is the one intelligible theory of the universe. "Matter," he holds, "is effete (hardened) mind, inveterate (engrained) habits becoming physical laws." To Peirce, matter was constructed out of habits of mind. The way we experience a brick, for instance, is just a habit of perception. In theory, it could change at any moment, but it has become so ingrained to be experienced in a certain way that it is all but impossible to break free of the assumption of solidity and to perceive it differently. According to Peirce, it was at least theoretically possible to see through the solidity of anything.

It was with a spirit of unbridled curiosity that Peirce approached the evolutionary ideas of Charles Darwin. Peirce and his friend William James both belonged to a discussion group of Harvard students and graduates that called itself The Metaphysical Club. It was in their club meetings that Peirce and James first began to develop the philosophical ideas that they would devote their respective lives to. And one of the central and ongoing concerns of the club was to debate, discuss and explore the implications of Darwin's Theory of Evolution by Natural Selection.

Peirce felt strongly that Darwin had not grasped the full extent of universal evolution. *On the Origin of Species* had only spoken about the evolution of animals and plants on Earth, but it did not account for the fact that the Earth itself, and the entire universe, must also have evolved into being. Darwin's theory describes a process of evolution that is contained on a single planet within the universe. Peirce would not accept that the process of evolution could have any container, because any container would itself have evolved. Even the seemingly immutable and eternal elements of the universe like time, space and causality must also have evolved. In an essay entitled *Design and Chance*, Peirce speculates as to how the seemingly everlasting elements of reality might have evolved into being.

Why must moments in time be ordered sequentially? He wondered. Maybe the first moments appeared in random order — one now, in the year 2020 — the next, ten days in the past — then, one four months in the future — then, one a thousand years in the past, and on and on. Perhaps those moments that happened, by chance, to appear in sequential order had a "survival advantage" and, eventually, all non-sequential moments had died out of existence. Maybe that is why we only find sequential moments in the universe today. And finding the universe as it is, we imagine that is how it must always have been.

The same may be true of space. It appears that all spots in space appear adjacent to one another. We never take a step in New York and find ourselves in Paris. But perhaps spots in space were not always arranged adjacently. Maybe the non-adjacent spots just died out over time.

And again, for causality; maybe things happened randomly initially and the habit of causality also developed gradually.

These are the kinds of common-sense-defying inquiries that Peirce's liberated and penetrating mind took seriously. His thought experiments give us a glimpse of how much of what we take for granted as "real", when considered more deeply, turns out to be unquestioned and unproven assumptions. Personally, I had a powerful awakening insight when I read the essay *Design and Chance*. As I followed the outlines of Peirce's inquiry, my sense of the solidity of the world melted away into a realization of its inherent fluidity. I saw, with blinding clarity, that the assumption of a hard and fast reality was just a mental habit that had stiffened over eons of time. I had learned to see a flowing reality as a collection of rigid moving parts.

You might wonder why sequential time, adjacent space and causality offer evolutionary advantages to the universe? To understand this, we must take another look at Peirce's semiotics. Remember, Peirce didn't see reality as something that exists independent of our understanding of it. Human understanding, and the words we use to describe reality, are themselves an extension of the reality they describe. The growth of understanding is the growth of the universe itself. Sequential time, adjacent space and causality make the universe more intelligible, and therefore an evolving universe naturally selects for them. For Peirce, human intelligibility is part of the ontological stuff of the universe. And our growing understanding of the universe is an important way in which the universe itself grows and expands. By the end of this chapter, we will see that Peirce eventually comes to the realization that the universe has a preference for growth.

In the essay *Design and Chance*, Peirce is mainly focused on determining the minimal preexisting characteristics that an evolving universe must have started with. These would be the true building blocks of reality. He settles on two characteristics. The first is spontaneous creation, pure chance, absolute novelty. In order for evolution to occur, there must be the possibility for something new to appear. Without this, nothing could ever have possibly arisen in the first place. But the possibility of novel occurrences is not enough, because a universe that contained only the ability for novelty would soon end up in total chaos with new and unrelated events continually exploding into existence in a never-ending cascade of confusion. The second essential characteristic that an evolving universe must possess is the ability to form habits. That means that once something has happened once, it becomes more likely for it to happen again. The tendency to form habits assures that there will be order in an evolving universe.

To put it simply, Peirce determined that an evolving universe must contain both the ability to change and the tendency to stick. Evolution proceeds as change that sticks. That's it. It was a simple and elegant description of the minimal ingredients required of an evolving universe.

The evolving universe begins with pure possibility from which things spontaneously burst into being. Once something appears once, it is more likely that it will happen again. Thus, the universe begins its evolutionary flow through events that happen, and then tend to happen again and again. And slowly, from nothing but pure possibility and a tendency toward habit, the universe grows. We have just journeyed through Peirce's original avenue of inquiry, to the idea that he would later expand upon and express in terms of Firstness, Secondness and Thirdness.

You will remember that Firstness is the essence of existence. Firstness is the quality that makes everything else possible. Secondness is the essence of contact. Secondness is what makes it possible to encounter another. Thirdness is the essence of relationship. Thirdness is what allows us to understand the qualities and characteristics of things.

As we saw in the last chapter, Peirce preferred to use the terms Firstness, Secondness and Thirdness in order to avoid making any unhelpful association with more common words he might have used. Unfortunately, this renders his description of evolution so hopelessly obscure that it tends to ward off all but the most ardent of readers. In my own studies, I found that my understanding of Peirce was helped along when I recognized some similarities between his ideas and the conception of "worlds" that was developed, decades later, by the German philosopher Martin Heidegger.

Heidegger made a distinction between the idea of the "universe" and the idea of the "world". Heidegger used the word universe to represent the entire domain of objective things, in much the same way that we most commonly use it. When he talked about worlds, however, he was referring exclusively to the domain of human meaning and significance that emerged out of our understanding of things. An example he used was a hammer. A hammer is not an object in the universe; it is a tool in the world. In the universe you have a wooden shank with a piece of metal on the end; a meaningless object without significance. Put that same object in a human world, among people who recognize what it is, and it becomes a hammer. Once it is a hammer, it can easily be used to bang nails into wood and build a house. In a culture that had no knowledge of what a hammer was, it would take a long time before someone might realize they could bang a nail with it, especially since they probably wouldn't know what nails were either.

Imagine a hammer that appears out of nowhere in the middle of a jungle with no one around. It exists, but it is not known or encountered. Now, imagine that someone who has no idea what a hammer is walks by, sees it and picks it up before throwing it back down onto the ground. The hammer has now been encountered, but it remains unknown. Finally imagine that a carpenter walks by, sees the hammer and places it in her tool kit. Now the hammer exists, is encountered, and is known.

It is my hope that you are developing an experiential understanding of Peirce's conceptions of Firstness, Secondness and Thirdness.

Firstness is pure existence. It means simply that a thing exists, but it is not known to exist. Secondness is contact. It means that something is known to exist, but nothing about it — other than the fact that it exists — is known. Thirdness is the world of understanding; it is everything that can be conceptualized about that which exists.

Notice the things around you. Look at something and call to mind everything you know about it. That is all Thirdness. What if you were to forget absolutely everything about it? What would it be then? You have stripped it of Thirdness and you are left in contact with something you know nothing about. If you turn away from the thing, you strip even the contact. What is left is just the existence of a thing, but of course we cannot even be sure that it still exists because we have no contact with it.

At this point you might be wondering why I didn't just say this in the first place. Why go through all the abstract explanation of Firstness, Secondness and Thirdness if we could just have explored it in this more directly experiential way? The reason is because this simpler way of talking about it does not give us access to the full depth of what Peirce was seeing. He would complain — as he often did about the philosophy of his friend William James — that taking this experiential view makes the world of Thirdness appear to exist only in the human mind. This would be a terrible misunderstanding of Peirce's evolutionary philosophy.

If we make the mistake of wedding Thirdness too tightly to human understanding, we miss the whole point. You see, in Peirce's philosophy there isn't a real physical hammer sitting there waiting for us to understand it. The hammer that we experience as a solid physical object is actually an idea that has been thought for so long, by so many beings, that it appears to exist as a solid object. If we are not very careful, we are likely to assume that Thirdness happens in human minds, but human beings are themselves habituated ideas of the even higher mental process of the universe.

To Peirce the universe was, in a sense, like a big mind and everything in it was an idea. The more habituated the idea, the more resistant it was to change or disappearance. Even we, ourselves, are created from habitual patterns of thought and feeling. We are not physical things; we are perceptual and mental patterns that have become habituated enough to appear solid. Again, it is useful to take yet another glance at the theory of semiotics that Peirce invented.

The concept of signs is so common to us that we hardly think about it. A sign is something that points to or indicates something else. We see signs all the time. Signs on stores, signs that direct us as we drive through traffic, signs are everywhere.

Peirce saw reality as nothing more than a constant exchange of signs. We do not experience reality directly; we experience signs of reality. Imagine that you see something on the ground a few feet in front of you that looks like a rock. You pick it up, and it feels like a rock. You toss it at a window, and it breaks through the glass like a rock. You conclude that if it looks like a rock, feels like a rock, and acts like a rock, it must be a rock.

But you never experienced a rock directly; you only experienced the signs of a rock. You saw things, felt things, and heard things that looked, sounded, and felt like a rock. And when you saw enough signs. you felt justified in your belief that there was actually a rock. But, in truth, you never saw a rock, you only ever experienced signs. You interpret the reality of the rock by reading signs. And, for Peirce, this is how reality works — not only for humans, but for everything.

Of course, it is a lot easier to understand this when we consider human-made artifacts. You see a building and on the building is a sign that says "Restaurant". Inside, you find tables and people sitting at them eating. You also find waiters, cooks and a cash register where money is being exchanged for the meals that are being eaten. You have seen enough signs to know that this is indeed a restaurant. But where exactly do you find the restaurant? You see signs of a restaurant, but signs of a restaurant are not actually a restaurant — just like signs of a rock are not actually a rock.

More intimately, the idea of signs relates to the search for the reality of our own self. When you apply this logic of signs to yourself, you are engaging in what is known as "pointing-out exercises" in the Buddhist tradition. You look for yourself, but you only find signs of a self. You find a body, you find memories, you find ideas about yourself and feelings that you are having, but you never find a self.

When considering the possibility that all of creation might be made only of signs pointing toward other signs, there might be a part of you that protests. It can't be signs all the way down. There has to be something real underneath all the signs. And, if you feel this way, you are feeling exactly the questions that were burning inside Peirce. What was it that was ultimately real, buried way down underneath all of the layers of signs? His conclusion was Firstness, the utterly inconceivable possibility of existence, and Secondness, the bare experience of contact, and finally Thirdness, the world of relationships that constitutes everything that we can know about.

In our contemporary materialistic culture, we have learned that the universe is made up of time, space, energy and matter. Peirce saw a universe that was entirely created from existence, contact, and relationships. Look around and see if you can see what Peirce saw: a universe where you don't see things, but instead you see signs of things. You see relationships; you see Thirdness all around you.

In his evolutionary philosophy, Peirce imagined that the universe begins as absolute Firstness — the pure possibility to exist, before anything has occurred. The ultimate destiny of the universe is to end with a magnificent completion experience of absolute Secondness — a final encounter with the absolute essence that initiated the creative process in the first place. Everything that happens in between these two extremes, which is the universe that we live in, is an unfolding of Thirdness — the ever-expanding growth of the relationships between things and the understanding about them.

Decades later, the French paleontologist and Jesuit priest, Pierre Teilhard de Chardin, would formulate his own evolutionary philosophy that included a vision of a final moment of total unification called the Omega Point. In an unsuccessful attempt to appease the church, Teilhard would describe his evolutionary vision using religious terminology. He explained how the universe starts with God, the ultimate potential of everything, and ends with a final encounter with God. Perhaps not surprisingly, we find that Teilhard had read Peirce's collected papers on a long train ride from his home in France to China where he had been effectively sent into exile by the church for his evolutionary views. But unlike Teilhard, Peirce believed the universe would never arrive at its destined finality because the end was forever being pushed further off into the future. As the amount of relationships and understanding continually grows, it generates more and more possibility for future relationships and more understanding, and so the final encounter never occurs.

As we have already explored, Peirce's earlier thinking about the nature of an evolving universe led him to see novelty and habit as the two absolutely necessary prerequisites to any process of evolution. He was puzzled, however, by the question of why the process of evolution seemed to be heading in a particular direction. Why did the universe prefer to be intelligible rather than incomprehensible? Why was anything preferable to anything else? Why did some habits stick and others not? Why did evolution seem to progress toward something? And ultimately, why did evolution start in the first place?

Peirce's answer to that question came to him as part of a spiritual realization. In a flash of insight, he saw that the path of evolution is guided by what he called the force of Agapism, or Evolutionary Love. This universal love is a tendency, in the universe, to "love" growth so much that it elicits a willingness to sacrifice for it. This tendency can be seen on perfect display in a mother's willingness to give so much to support the growth and well-being of her child.

In an essay called *Evolutionary Love*, written in 1893, Peirce captures the essence of what he meant by Agapism in a sentence which reflects some of Emerson's ideas — specifically, the view that evolution proceeds through a process of splintering off pieces and then reuniting them.

"The movement of love is circular, at one and the same impulse projecting creations into independency and drawing them into harmony."

For Peirce, Agapism or Evolutionary Love is the essential dynamic of all creative growth. It is the fundamental pattern that drives all of evolution, and it is composed of two seemingly opposing impulses that work together. One impulse drives new creations out into existence; the other draws them back into harmonious union with what came before. It is a process of birthing and nurturing, of transcending and including. When looked at from the right vantage point, it becomes apparent that all of this evolutionary energy tends unhesitatingly toward the one thing that evolution loves — growth.

Peirce's lifelong friend, William James, was also a scientist and a philosopher, but he was not a hard scientist like Peirce — he was a psychologist. Over the course of his life, James would work on his own theory to describe the nature of reality and the mechanisms of its evolution. Where Peirce's writings are infamously technical and obtuse, James was said to write psychology texts like a novelist and he wrote philosophy in ways that could be popularly understood. In our next chapter, we will begin to explore James' thinking.

CHAPTER SEVEN

The Field of Consciousness

William James started discussing philosophy with Charles Sanders Peirce in the 1860s, and the two continued to engage in philosophical discourse until James' death in 1910. Both of their fathers were close associates of Ralph Waldo Emerson and the circle of Concord transcendentalists. We have just explored how Peirce's thinking included a conception of essence, or what he called Firstness, that was in many ways similar to Emerson's idea of the soul. In this chapter, we will explore William James' idea of the field of consciousness. We will find congruence with Peirce and we will see how James' expression of ideas is more tightly bound to the human experience.

James began his career as a psychologist and his primary drive was toward understanding the human experience rather than creating a coherent universal cosmology (the way Peirce had been driven to do). James worked out many of his core ideas while writing his masterwork *The Principles of Psychology* — which took 10 years to write and was published in 1890. Many of the profound insights he articulated about psychology would continue to propagate and reverberate throughout his entire career as a philosopher as well.

We will begin our story with a comparison of two daringly original thinkers; contemporaries working on opposite sides of the Atlantic Ocean. One is William James and the other is Rudolf Steiner — who published his doctoral thesis entitled *A Theory of Knowledge Implicit in Goethe's World Conception* in 1886. Both men independently developed philosophies founded in the recognition that the world always presents itself as impressions of direct experience that cannot be qualified in any way. In essence, the philosophies of both James and Steiner begin with the assumption that reality first appears to us as a multitude of unintelligible first impressions. In the following passage, Steiner describes the reality of pure experience in words that could just as easily have been written by James.

> Let us now take a look at pure experience. What does it contain, as it sweeps across our consciousness, without our working upon it in thinking? It is mere juxtaposition in space and succession in time; an aggregate of utterly disconnected particulars. None of the objects that come and go there has anything to do with any other. At this stage, the facts that we perceive, that we experience inwardly, are of no consequence to each other. This world is a manifoldness of things of equal value. No thing or event can claim to play a greater role in the functioning of the world than any other part of the world of experience. If it is to become clear to us that this or that fact has greater significance than another one, we must then not merely observe the things, but must already bring them into thought-relationships.

In order for our pure experiences to take on qualities or find themselves in relationship with each other, a second element must act upon them; that element is thought or reason. The process of thought attributes qualities to pure experiences, relates some experiences to other experiences, and builds an intelligibly conceptualized world.

Thinking is a process that emerges spontaneously in order to arrange and qualify experience. The process of thought proceeds not from our conscious direction, but in accordance with what Steiner referred to as organic laws of interconnection. These laws are part of the nature of reality and not within our control. In other words, thinking isn't something we do, it's something that happens.

Pure experience presents itself in a relentless succession of unintelligible impressions. Thoughts grow out of experience, qualifying it and situating it in relationship to other experiences. The process of thinking is not an activity that we perform. Thoughts, we could say, emerge out of pure experience in the way grass appears out of the ground. Ralph Waldo Emerson expressed a similar sentiment when he called thinking "a second nature that grows out of the first like a leaf grows out of a tree."

Over the course of his lifetime, William James worked to develop a philosophy founded on the assumption that reality is created entirely from pure experience; it is a field of consciousness. James' conception of this field holds many similarities to Coleridge and Emerson's vision of reason and the human soul, and to Peirce's conception of Firstness.

James' field of consciousness is a background of pure intelligence that all thought and feeling emerges out of. Like Emerson and Coleridge, James believed that all of human intelligence emerges from the same universal source. This point of view raises a challenging philosophical question, especially for a psychologist. If all human intelligence comes from the same source, why do we experience ourselves as separate individuals?

Emerson and Coleridge were more comfortable with the dualistic split between mind and matter. They were satisfied to believe that there was one universal mind, and that mind divided as it expressed itself through individual human bodies. James, however, was unwilling to accept that reality was split between mind and matter. He believed that both mind and matter were made of pure experience, the only real stuff in the universe.

If reality is ultimately a field of consciousness, then what makes me "me" and not "you"? Why do I think my thoughts and not yours? How am I able to make choices that appear to be free and uniquely mine, when behind it all, I am animated by the same field of consciousness that you are?

These were the kinds of questions that James asked and, by pursuing them, came to an understanding of human consciousness that helped him explain what we are and how we can transform.

James believed that what makes my experience different from yours is that there are different habitual patterns of attention that exists within the same field of consciousness. I have become habituated to holding my attention only on a certain area in the field of consciousness, and you in another. The area within the field of consciousness we have learned to focus on is different for each of us, and this is what creates the individuality of our personality.

Imagine all of reality as a field of pure experience. Different thoughts and feelings emerge out of different locations within this field. James realized that each of us draws a line around a certain area of the field, and the experiences that lie inside that particular demarcation are the ones I call "me", while those that lie outside of that boundary, I call the "world" or the "other". In *The Principles of Psychology*, he writes with lucid clarity about how each of us creates a unique sense of self by separating ourselves out of the larger unified whole of which we are a part.

> One great splitting of the whole universe into two halves is made by each of us; and for each of us almost all of the interest attaches to one of the halves; but we all draw the line of division between them in a different place. When I say that we all call the two halves by the same names, and that those names are 'me' and 'not-me' respectively, it will at once be seen what I mean. The altogether unique kind of interest which each human mind feels in those parts of creation which it can call me or mine may be a moral riddle, but it is a fundamental psychological fact. No mind can take the same interest in his neighbour's me as in his own. The neighbour's me falls together with all the rest of things in one foreign mass against which his own me stands cut in startling relief... He is for me a mere part of the world; for him it is I who am the mere part. Each of us dichotomizes the Kosmos in a different place.

As James explains above, the line we draw that separates us from the rest of reality defines our primary circle of concern. We care more about what lies within the boundary of self than with what lies outside the boundary that defines us. In short, we ourselves define a sphere of concern that then dictates what we care about, what shapes our choices and ultimately, defines who we are. The experiences that lie within our sphere of concern are energetically alive to us, and this energy is what gives them the feeling of belonging to us.

As a psychologist, James was compelled to understand how people change. Throughout his life, he attempted to create a philosophy of transformation that was consistent with his understanding of how reality emerges out of a field of pure experiences. He believed that human transformation happens when our habitual sphere of concern moves and expands. Through this process, we are able to shift and increase what we care about by changing the boundary that defines us. As a man of moral sensibilities, James saw mastering the art of self-transformation and expanding our sphere of concern as an ethical imperative.

In his most famous book, *The Varieties of Religious Experience*, James outlines his theory of self-development. He first states that a life is moral "in proportion as it is less swayed by paltry personal considerations and more by objective ends that call for energy, even though that energy brings personal loss and pain." For him, the direction of moral goodness is in a greater willingness to sacrifice in order to accomplish universal aims. In other words, our ability to dedicate ourselves consistently to the betterment of a greater whole is the measure of our moral goodness.

In this same book, James describes the transformation of the self as a process of unification that can be either gradual or sudden. Human beings are divided between a host of different temptations and impulses that all coexist within our sphere of concern. In extreme cases, the antagonism between different impulses within our sphere of concern causes psychosis, but in truth, we are all divided to some degree by the competing motives within our sphere of concern.

According to James, the fundamental mechanism of psychological or spiritual growth is chiefly a matter of the straightening out and unifying of the inner self. James describes how each of us must struggle to unify our self around higher and nobler aims and ideals.

> The higher and the lower feelings, the useful and the erring impulses, begin by being a comparative chaos within us — they must end by forming a stable system of functions in right subordination... The man's interior is a battle-ground for what he feels to be two deadly hostile selves, one actual, the other ideal.

James spends two chapters exploring the phenomenon of religious conversion. The mystery of the transformation that occurs in the self through a religious conversion was a central concern for

James because such conversions offer the most dramatic examples of the true transformative potential of human beings. He studied hundreds of cases of religious conversion, noting each time and with great fascination that the person who emerged out of the transformation was, at least temporarily, a different person from the one that entered into it.

What is it that occurs when a person undergoes a gradual or sudden shift in perspective significant enough to turn them into a dramatically different person — sometimes permanently?

In the first chapter on conversion, James states clearly the general psychological thesis from which he starts his investigations into this phenomenon. "A man's ideas, aims, and objects," he writes, "form diverse internal groups and systems, relatively independent of one another." James, as one of the early pioneers of psychology, understands how our inner mental workings are grouped into systems orbiting around one another without necessarily relating well to other systems of ideas inside us. These mental spheres of related ideas all float in the field of consciousness like solar systems in space.

James believed that we all experience the mechanism of transformation in small ways every day. Intentions arise in us throughout the day, enlivening certain mental spheres that are called into the service of fulfilling some desired objective. Under the influence of a strong intention or desire, the mental spheres associated with that intent dominate our attention so that we become temporarily blind to other systems of ideas, systems that have been effectively pushed out of consciousness. For example, I might be in the middle of working when a craving for chocolate arises. Suddenly, I find myself hunting through the cabinets searching for the last piece of chocolate that I know is somewhere. I have temporarily forgotten all about what I was doing, but I will return to it as soon as my craving for chocolate is filled. To James, such a miniature transformation shows us how the process of transformation in general always works.

These instances of focused intention are common to all of us. Under the influence of a strong intention, we become focused on the aim of our intention and we become hyperaware of those parts of ourselves and the world that will serve us in achieving it.

These shifts are not ordinarily considered transformations because the duration of the change is short-lived and soon replaced by another. But these common examples of shifting attention do show us the fundamental mechanism of transformation which James describes as occurring "whenever one aim grows so stable as to expel definitively its previous rivals from the individual's life, we tend to speak of the phenomenon, and perhaps to wonder at it, as a 'transformation.'"

James spoke of our experience of reality as occurring in "a succession of fields of consciousness." He envisioned our experience as a field that extends out infinitely. At any given moment, we are only conscious of some portion of that field and the rest of it lies outside of our conscious awareness.

Within the conscious part of the field there is always:

> (...) a sub-field, which figures as focal and contains the excitement, and from which, as from a centre, the aim seems to be taken. Talking of this part, we involuntarily apply words of perspective to distinguish it from the rest, words like 'here,' 'this,' 'now,' 'mine,' or 'me; — and we ascribe to the other parts the positions 'there,' 'then, ' 'that,' 'his' or 'thine,' 'it,' 'not me.'

This sub-field feels different to us. It is closer, more immediate, and of greater concern to us than any of the other things that we might also be aware of. James referred to it as the "hot spot" in consciousness because experiences that occur within that sub-field compel us to respond to them with greater intensity.

We experience the hot part of our consciousness as the center of our awareness and the seat of our volition, in contrast to the colder parts of consciousness that do not spur us to action and instead "leave us indifferent and passive in proportion to their coldness."

We all have different interests and desires, and they all seem to compete within us as one interest after another comes to dominate attention for a period of time until its aim is complete. This is the ordinary state of the divided self. James realized that a permanent transformation of the self takes place when one intention becomes so dominant in consciousness that the constant shifting within the self comes to an end. The self has become unified rather than divided. When this shift of unification is of a religious nature, centered on a spiritual concern, James called it a conversion.

James explained the psychology of transformation in terms of a shift in the habitual center of a person's personal energy. For someone to be converted means "that religious ideas, previously peripheral in his consciousness, now take a central place, and that religious aims form the habitual center of his energy." The spiritually transformed individual is now centered on a spiritual intention that guides his or her choices and actions.

As a psychologist James was fascinated by the mechanisms of human transformation. As we just described, James saw how the sphere of concern that defines our self exists within the larger field of consciousness, and that it grows both by expanding at its edges and shifting its center to new locations.

As a philosopher, James saw a universe of pure experience that was filled with hot spots of selfhood that grew and moved about, expanding at their edges and becoming more and more interconnected and overlapping. From a human point of view, our individual experience of ourselves and the world continually grows, and as we grow, our experience touches and merges with the experience of others. We gradually become more unified through shared experience. What James saw was a universe of centers of perception that were becoming ever more unified. In his essay, A World of Pure Experience, he called the world, "a pluralism of which the unity is not fully experienced as yet," adding that, "... the universe continually grows in quantity by new experiences that graft themselves upon the older mass; but these very new experiences often help the mass to a more consolidated form."

As a psychologist, James' writing reflected a human point of view, a fact that his friend Charles Sanders Peirce was known to complain about. For instance, even in the quotations I have used in this chapter, when James says, "One great splitting of the whole universe into two halves is made by each of us..." or "The man's interior is a battle-ground..." or "...we involuntarily apply words..." he seems to be referring to things that we, human beings, are doing within the field of consciousness. This would make it appear that we existed separate from it, swimming around in it like an ocean.

I don't believe that James did see reality that way. He didn't want to replace an image of *people existing in a physical universe that we were separate from* with a new image of *people living in a field of consciousness that we were separate from* — even if he did, at times, use language that might imply that.

The grand philosophical vision that James was working on, but never finished, was called radical empiricism, and one of the things that this theory asserted was that the world, and everything in it, was created out of pure experience. Pure experience was the only actual "stuff" in existence.

From this point of view, we ourselves are not physical beings that exist inside a field of consciousness that develops habits of limited perception. The experience of being us is nothing more than a set of habits of perception. There is nothing else to us.

Our body is not a physical thing, it is a set of stubbornly habituated perceptions of having a body. We ourselves are also not a thing, we are another set of stubborn habits of thinking that we exist. If we look for ourselves, all we will ever find is more experience. I can look at my body, call memories to mind, admire my qualities, but all I will be doing is having experiences. Experiences of a body, experiences of remembering, experiences of admiring. Everything, including ourselves, is made up of pure experience. As an interesting side note, James' idea was brought to Kitaro Nishida who founded the Japanese Kyoto School of Zen Buddhism. Nishida was so taken by James' articulation of pure experience that he made it a central part of the philosophy of the Kyoto School.

If we look closely, we can see a deep similarity between James' vision of reality and that of his friend Charles Sanders. In the essay *A World of Pure Experience,* James describes the nature of reality as consisting of "...a conscious field plus its object as felt or thought of plus an attitude towards the object plus the sense of a self to whom the attitude belongs."

If we were to substitute the term Firstness in place of "a conscious field", and then replace the "object as felt" with Secondness, and finally let Thirdness stand in place of "an attitude towards the object plus the sense of a self," we would see that James is working out an articulation of a theory very similar to that of Charles

Sanders Peirce. James may talk about people having centers of interest in a field of consciousness, but we have to remember that the person who has such a center is themselves made up of only habits of experience.

As James worked to complete his philosophy of radical empiricism, he repeatedly ran into two challenging problems that he wrote extensively about. We will devote one chapter to each of these gnarly problems because they figured so prominently in James' thinking and because they shaped the thinking of American philosophers for years to come. The problems James wrestled with were: the question of free will and notion of truth.

CHAPTER EIGHT

Free Will

In this chapter, we are going to explore the question of human free will, or lack thereof, which was a central concern for William James. His friend Charles Sanders Peirce doesn't seem to have been as bothered by the question; perhaps because, as we have already discussed, Peirce saw the universe as inherently free and creative at its very core. How that freedom propagated into the human experience wasn't something that he seems to have been overly concerned with. James, on the other hand, spent a great deal of energy pondering this age-old question.

Generally speaking, the question of free will arises for us because we see that there are so many factors influencing, and ultimately determining, what is possible for us that it makes us wonder if we have any freedom of choice at all. James struggled with the idea of free will for exactly this reason, and the question was fueled for him by his background as a psychologist and his knowledge of all the inner drives and attitudes that shape our decisions and opinions.

 But we will also see in this chapter that the question of free will, for James, is spurred by deeper and more profound concerns. Specifically, James' commitment to a unified universe called into question the very existence of human beings as separate entities that would even be possible of exercising freedom. What we are about to see is how a question like, "Do human beings have free will?" inevitably leads us into the most subtle and complex philosophical terrain. The question itself sounds straightforward, but you don't have to look into it very long to realize that it sits on a mountain of other ideas and assumptions that need to be addressed before we can even understand what the question is asking.

One of the things that James realized was that, before you can tackle the question of human free will, you have to think long and hard about what it means to be human in the first place. What is a human being? Peirce and James were committed to a vision of a continuous universe. Human beings, therefore, could not be objects that exist in a universe that is separate from us. The demand of unity is that we must find a way to understand the human experience that does not contradict our utter inseparability from the universe as a whole. We have to see ourselves as a part of the universe in the same way that an ocean wave is an inseparable part of the ocean.

It is common today for people to think in terms of the "interconnectedness" of all things. But even that term falls short of being able to express what the early American philosophers were pointing toward, because it implies a collection of separate elements that are connected and not one continuous whole.

Another image that has helped me grasp the demands of unity is an air bubble in water. The idea of taking the bubble out of the water is nonsensical. A bubble is defined by the water around it. The idea of a bubble has no meaning outside of the context of water. In the same way, a human being is defined by its environment, by the world if you will, and the idea of removing the human being from the world is equally nonsensical.

The layer of life around the Earth is referred to as the biosphere, and if you think about it, a human being — from one perspective — can be thought of as a bubble in the biosphere like an air bubble in water. If, for instance, you were to want to remove an air bubble from a pond, you would have to use a container (like a jar) that would hold enough water for the bubble to be held in. Similarly, if you want to remove a human from the biosphere, you have to create a container (like a spaceship) that would hold enough biosphere for the human to be held in. In the last chapter, we explained how James saw our own habits of mind existing as an inseparable part of the larger field of consciousness. Teilhard de Chardin would later coin the term noosphere to describe the sphere of global mental activity that permeates the biosphere.

Getting back to the problem of free will, we have all learned to think of ourselves as separate entities. So, we naturally tend to think of free will as a quality or an attribute of ourselves. What we will see in this chapter is that James ultimately determined that the question of whether or not human beings have free will was a question of perspective. From inside the experience of being a human being, it looks like we have free will; from the outside perspective of the universe, what we experience as free choices, are really the end results of chains of influence that we cannot see. Every wave on the ocean crests differently as it approaches the shore, but that doesn't mean that every wave chooses how it will break even if it were to happen to feel that way to the wave.

Maybe the relationship between free will and human beings is more similar to the relationship between sight and eyes, between a capacity and the instrument that allows that capacity to come into being. Can eyes see? Of course not, eyes are simply the organ of perception that allow the whole human being to see. Do human beings have free will? Of course not, the human being is simply the organ of choice that allows the universe to express its capacity for novelty.

My reading of James and Peirce leads me to see freedom as a fundamental characteristic of the universe rather than of human beings. It is inherent in the spontaneity of Firstness that Peirce wrote about. It manifests in human beings as our ability to make choices, but it is not a characteristic of a human being; it is a characteristic of the universe as a whole. By way of analogy, when a friend talks to me, the words emerge from her mouth, but I don't think that her mouth is talking. I know that she is talking. The intelligence that is expressed in the words is not a characteristic of her mouth. The intelligence is hers.

Let's look at a quote from the German philosopher Arthur Schopenhauer, from his most famous book *The World as Will and Idea:*

> *Spinoza says that if a stone which has been projected through the air had consciousness, it would believe that it was moving of its own will. I add to this only that the stone would be right. The impulse given it is for the stone what the motive is for me, and what in the case of the stone appears as cohesion,*

gravitation, rigidity, is in its inner nature the same as that
which I recognize in myself as will, and what the stone also,
if knowledge were given to it, would recognize as will.

Is it possible that we are like that stone flying through the air?
We find ourselves propelled through an evolving universe within
which everything, including us, is constantly changing. We see
ourselves changing, we see the things we come in contact with
changing, and we think, "I am changing", "I am making things
change". We assume that the changes we see in ourselves and the
things we touch are a result of our own will and intention, but
where does our will and intention come from? We assume that
"we are generating change", when in fact, change is propagating
through us from a source beyond our awareness. We see change
happening in the universe, and from our perspective, it *feels* like
we are doing things, when in fact it is all just stuff happening.

After all, isn't the main reason we believe so strongly in the
existence of free will simply because it feels like we make free
choices. But aren't our choices always influenced? A young man
may decide he wants to be a doctor and he may feel that it is a
decision he made according to the dictates of his own free will.
But if we find out that his father, his father's father, and his
father's father's father were all also doctors, we might wonder
how free that choice really was. Is there not some aspect of family
expectation playing a role in the choosing? Many Americans
love cheeseburgers, many Indians love dhal and many Israelis
love salad with olives for breakfast. Are these free choices, or
are they culturally conditioned? Aren't all the choices that we
make, and the range of options open to us, limited by the physical
characteristics of our bodies, the mental qualities of our minds
and the environmental circumstances that have shaped us? How
free is our will?

Charles Sanders Peirce and William James were the founders
of the American philosophy of pragmatism, and the essence of
that philosophy is an assertion about truth that states that the
only real difference between competing ideas is what difference
it makes to believe in one versus the other. The only thing that
matters about an idea is the difference it makes to believe in it.
In the case of free will, we would ask what difference it makes
if we believe that we have free will or not. If we believe in free

will, do we have a deeper sense of creative power? Do we become more productive human beings? Or, on the other hand, if we don't believe in free will, does it make it easier for us to feel victimized and give up responsibility?

William James' obsessive engagement with questions of free will may have started with the question of whether we have free will or not, but eventually, he became even more concerned with the potential significance of believing that we do. In the end, he concluded that it wasn't even possible to authentically doubt our own free will, because even that question would feel to us like something we were choosing to engage with.

James was a psychologist, and so he knew that our choices were the result of a complex array of influences of our own unconscious minds and the impact of our surroundings. In fact, he believed that our deep emotional predispositions had more influence over our choices than any rational or logical decision-making process. James believed that each of us has, at our core, one of two fundamental temperaments. We are either "tough-minded" or "tender-minded." The tough-minded among us are scientifically inclined individuals who believe in the power of empirical facts and logic. Those that are tender-minded are romantically inclined and trust in the sensitivities of intuition and emotion.

What was so insightful in this distinction was James' recognition that it is our tough or tender predisposition that dictate our opinions and determine our actions. We are all trained to see ourselves as logical individuals who come to decisions and form opinions rationally. We believe that when we make a decision or form an opinion, we do so by looking at reality and then logically coming to a conclusion about what we see. But James believed that a "tough-minded" person and a "tender-minded" person will look at exactly the same reality and come to two completely different conclusions, and both will explain their conclusion in logical terms that make sense to them. But here is the point, the decision or the opinion was not formed logically, it was an inevitable outcome of our inner temperament. We don't use logic to come to decisions and form opinions. We use logic to explain and justify them afterward. Where is the free will in that? Perhaps James himself said it best when he stated, "A great many people think they are thinking when they are merely rearranging their prejudices."

In the last chapter of his masterwork, *The Principles of Psychology,* James states that — as a science — psychology must assume that human actions and attitudes are generated through a deterministic process that is directed by perceptions and the relationships between them, and not by an entity that has the power of free will.

James developed an important theory of emotion, which today is called the James-Lange theory, named after the two people who developed it independently. The theory states that our emotions start as imperceptible bodily movements. If we see something frightening, our body begins to get tense, our temperature rises and our heart beats faster. The mind sees these responses and interprets them as fear, but it is the bodily responses that come first, the sense of emotion second. To put it another way, if we see a dangerous animal we do not run because we are scared, we are scared because we see ourselves running.

Now, if the action of running was an involuntary instinctive reaction that occurred before we even realized we were afraid, then who chose to run? James saw our actions starting as an imperceptible dance of perception and reaction. Our eyes see and our bodies respond to what is seen before our mind knows what's happening. A finger pulls away from a flame before we have even felt the burn. Anger flares up before we fully understand what our colleague just said. Everything is just happening, and our poor brains are working so hard alongside it all, desperately trying to maintain a plausible narrative that describes everything in terms of things that we are doing and choices we are making.

There is a very interesting moment when the imperceptible reaction of our bodies first becomes conscious to our mind. We were not aware of the subtle movements — mental or physical — that precipitated that moment, and so it feels like the action started at that moment. We have learned to interpret that moment as the one that we chose to do something, but was it? Or was that just the moment that we became aware of a process that had already begun?

The question of free will for James was just the tip of the iceberg of a much bigger question. Before we can even consider asking the question of whether or not we have free will, we have to tackle the question of whether or not we exist at all. James didn't believe that we did. James believed in a world of pure experience. He believed that we only existed as a set of stubborn perceptual habits. So how could someone who didn't exist have free will? James, like Peirce, believed in a universe without separation or division. That means there cannot be a person that exists separate from the field of consciousness, so there is no person who could be making free choices.

James was trained as a medical doctor at Harvard University and became generally recognized as the first psychologist in America. In *The Principles of Psychology*, James writes about the stream of consciousness and he lays out his theory for how the sense of self is created where none actually exists.

James saw consciousness as a stream consisting of a continuous succession of experiences; an unending parade of thoughts, feelings, images, ideas, sensations, conceptions and emotions that appear to conscious awareness and then pass away. But James also recognized that the lines dividing these apparently separate objects of consciousness were not as sharp as we, at first, might assume. In fact, he realized that if each of our experiences was entirely unique and separate from those that came before and those that would come later, we would live in a chaos of random disconnected experiences.

Instead of this chaos, our experience is of a continuous stream of consciousness that presents no breaks or gaps. We seem to flow from one moment to the next without any sense of break or division. The last thought or feeling we experienced is part of a stream that includes our current thought and those yet to come. In fact, all of our thoughts, feelings and sensations — yesterday's, today's and every day's — are recognized to be part of the same river of awareness. According to James, our cognitive experiences overlap so that each experience has "fringes" that reach out on both ends. One fringe leaning out into the future and another lagging behind in the past. Our present experience is always the most obvious to us, but the tail ends of our past experiences are still a part of this moment, and the leading edges of future moments of experience are already beginning to enter our awareness now.

James had an intriguing vision for how the process of consciousness, including the process of thinking, can go on in a line that looks intelligently directed, but does not require the existence of any independent entity that could be called a "thinker". Thinking is a goal-oriented process and what propels our thinking forward is not a person directing it, but rather an attraction toward the feeling of satisfaction that builds as each thought moves us closer to the goal. James imagined thinking as a purely automated process guided by a force of attraction without anyone controlling or directing it. Our thoughts move toward final conclusions because of an attractive force that pulls them toward a goal. This attractive force of mind is like the attractive force of gravity. The force of gravity makes things fall in straight lines without anyone directing them. The process of cognition can carry on without any separate person to guide it. As human beings, we mistakenly see ourselves as the guiding force of our thought process, when in fact it is a completely automated process led by the desire to experience satisfaction.

James believed that our sense of self — the feeling that we have of being someone who exists — is also automatically produced within the stream of consciousness. He explained that, within the stream of consciousness, we have experiences of things outside of ourselves, and then we have experiences of an abstract image of ourselves having those experiences. We see a tree, then we imagine ourselves seeing the tree. Next, we see ourselves taking a step and we imagine ourselves walking. Experiences of the world, and imagined experiences of us in the world, are interspersed within the stream of consciousness. This is what gives us the sense that we exist when in fact the only thing that exists is a succession of experiences — an unending parade of thoughts, feelings, images, ideas, sensations, conceptions and emotions. Some of those experiences picture an imagined sense of self that we then think is who we are.

James' training as a psychologist, and his belief in a world of pure experience, led him unerringly to the conclusion that human free will could not exist because human beings — at least as separate entities — do not exist. But this was not his final word on the topic.

In an essay called *Are we Automatons?* James tackles the question of free will directly. His conclusion: We are not automatons! We are a selecting organ. And while we may not have the ability to consciously select what objects appear to our awareness, we do have the power to continue to pay attention to them or not. Those mental objects that we choose to give our attention to inevitably express themselves in our choices and opinions, but we always have the freedom not to pay attention.

In spite of the fact that his psychological training and ontological convictions pointed to determinism, James was a firm believer in free will. His personal conviction in free will did not come from evidence or data, however, it was born out of a dark time in his life. In 1870, James found himself in the midst of a crisis that pushed him to the verge of suicide, but in his darkest hour, he decided that he would conduct an experiment. He would devote one year to proving to himself that he could, through willful effort, improve his lot and change. He would prove to himself that free will did indeed exist. In his diary he wrote, "I will assume for the present — until next year — that it is no illusion. My first act of free will shall be to believe in free will." Some biographers see this moment of awakening as the guiding inspiration for the rest of his life.

In one of James' most important essays, *The Will to Believe*, he makes a case for the fact that the place we can exercise our will is in choosing which ideas we believe in. Our beliefs inevitably lead to action and ultimately to consequences in the world, so we must be very careful to exercise our will to believe carefully. Believing in the will to believe gave James an enormous amount of faith in human potential. By learning to control where we put our attention and choosing what we believe, we are capable of accomplishing almost anything.

In short, we may not be an entity with free will, but we do seem to play a role within the field of consciousness that exercises the power to focus attention in one spot or another, and from that sustained focus miracles can unfold.

CHAPTER NINE

The Nature of Truth

The two founders of pragmatism, Charles Sanders Peirce and William James, both wanted to describe the nature of reality, and they were both seeing reality dramatically differently than most people believed it was. Because they wanted to explain this strange new reality, they realized they would need to help people open their minds wide enough to be able to see what they saw. James, in particular, was focused on finding ways to open people's minds. He particularly wanted people to break the habit of narrow mindedness that he called vicious intellectualism.

Peirce and James believed that reality was fundamentally non-material, and for many thinkers of the time, that was an utterly unacceptable position to hold. Some of the greatest opposition these two "scientists turned philosophers" had to face came from the scientific community itself because, by the late nineteenth century, science was rapidly consolidating a view of reality that was becoming indisputable. It was a materialistic vision of a universe made up of a vast expanse of empty space, filled with material objects that were themselves made up of tiny particles. Everything that occurred within and between pieces of matter was governed by a handful of fundamental forces and energy. Peirce and James were both scientists, and both admired and appreciated the power of science. At the same time, they saw the limitations of the scientific point of view, especially if it became the only point of view. What Peirce and James were battling was what today we would call scientism.

Science is a method of inquiry involving hypothesis and experimentation designed to lead to theories about how the world works and improve human life. Science is also the body of knowledge gained through the scientific method.

Scientism is the belief that everything that science determines to be true, must in fact be true.

Peirce and James were pro-science and anti-scientism, and their passionate insistence that we must look beyond the assumptions of materialism to find the truth probably originated with one of their early mentors, Chauncey Wright. Wright was a staunch materialist and a member of the same metaphysical club in Cambridge that included James and Peirce.

Wright was the elder statesman of the metaphysical club, and it was against his keen intellect that Peirce and James first sharpened their own thinking. In club meetings, members would engage in dynamic discussion and Wright was seen as a master of inquiry and debate. And one of the things that Wright felt strongly about was that, in describing reality, we should never resort to assuming any supernatural or metaphysical influences. Reality, he believed, had to be explained in terms of real elements that were observably evident. Essentially, Wright believed that reality was made up of a collection of quantifiable empirical facts. The cosmos was like the weather — a phenomenon created through the interaction of elements. There is no need to appeal to any supernatural entities or metaphysical principles to explain the changes in the weather, and there should be none needed to explain the workings of the universe either.

Wright was a scientific materialist of the kind that both Peirce and James would spend a great deal of their life's energy trying to discredit or at least question. At the same time, both Peirce and James were deeply influenced by Wright and embraced his insistence that no supernatural or metaphysical assumptions should enter into our explanations of ultimate truth. They spent their lifetimes working out visions of a unified, whole, non-dual reality that evolved without a metaphysical god-like entity or a transcendent self.

James and Peirce knew that reality was vastly different than what we thought, and probably it would always be different than anything we could ever know. They were passionately driven by a recognition that what we know about reality, and even what we can imagine about it, is trivial compared to the totality of what is real. As a result, they envisioned a way of doing philosophy that was relentlessly open-ended.

"Never block the road to inquiry" was Peirce's motto, and of course, thinking that you already know what is true is one of the surest ways to block the road of inquiry. At the heart of Peirce's philosophy was what he called the doctrine of fallibilism, which simply means that any of our current beliefs, no matter how certain we are about them, might be wrong.

If you think about it for a moment, how could it be otherwise?

Here we are, living on a single planet revolving around a single star in a galaxy that contains trillions of stars. The galaxy, within which we are smaller than a speck, is itself only one of trillions of galaxies in the universe. We have access to the perceptual senses of only one biological form, and we have knowledge of a mere few thousand years of our own history.

We know that our eyes only see a tiny fragment of the electromagnetic spectrum, and our ears only hear a tiny amount of the sound around us, but we don't have any way of knowing how minuscule a portion of the universe we have access to. It seems likely that what we are currently aware of is virtually insignificant.

In short, we only know what we know, and there is no way to know how small a portion of the whole that is, or what might lie beyond our current ability to imagine or cognize.

There are things that we know. There are things that we know that we don't know. And there are things that we don't know that we don't know. Peirce and James were both very concerned with the realm of the unknown unknowns. Both realized that human beings find it very difficult to imagine that there are things that we don't even know that we don't know. We know there are things that we don't know. I don't know lots of scientific and cultural facts, the distance to the nearest star, the president of Monaco and so on. But I know that these are facts I could know.

Those things that we don't know that we don't know, lay so far outside of our existing frame of reference that we can't even imagine their existence. We cannot even conceive of the possibility of them. What endears me to pragmatism, more than anything else, is the respect given to the existence of truths beyond our current ability to imagine — and this was exactly what spurred William James to describe and confront what he called vicious intellectualism.

Vicious intellectualism, as James explained it, was the conscious or unconscious assumption that the affirmation of any statement of truth automatically implied the negation of all alternative possibilities. In many mundane situations, this is a perfectly safe assumption. For instance, if I see something and say that is blue, it is perfectly reasonable and safe to assume that it is not red, yellow, green, or any other color.

One of the reasons James was so bothered by vicious intellectualism was that he saw how severely limiting it was to our imagination. If we assume that what we believe is true and negate any contradictory possibilities, we won't ever even consider any alternative points of view. James' passion around this is partially connected to his fears around the dominance of the scientific worldview. James had serious doubts about the ability of science to understand all of reality. By the late 19th century, science had proven its prowess in many areas of life, but James was concerned that science was becoming the sole arbiter of truth.

James was fascinated by many things that lay outside of the bounds of science. He was the president of the American Psychical Society and had a keen interest in the study of the paranormal. The scientific establishment dismissed such studies, but James saw this offhanded dismissal as very unscientific. James believed that we should not ignore things just because they defy our current scientific understanding; in fact, that is the very reason we should study them — because they are giving us a clear indication that we have more to learn.

The habit of vicious intellectualism makes it difficult for us to see beyond what we already know. The unconscious tendency to assume that anything that contradicts our current understanding of truth is wrong, blocks the road to inquiry because it makes us resistant to considering alternative possibilities. As James saw it, with an imagination hampered by vicious intellectualism, our growth in understanding can only proceed by slowly expanding at the edges of what we already know. The process of discovery will always move at a snail's pace because there will never be much willingness to investigate potentially revolutionary possibilities.

James and Peirce wanted to liberate our thinking. They encouraged us to hold our current beliefs loosely, knowing that whatever we think is true now will yield tomorrow to a new and more encompassing truth. James very directly wanted us to stop spending so much energy defending what we already know, and instead, be willing to inquire directly into things that were already calling our assumptions into question. He promoted the idea that understanding proceeds more rapidly if we are willing to focus on the anomalies and oddities that don't fit into our current understanding.

James wanted us to give more of our attention to the outer fringes of what we know. The next big idea doesn't come from the center. It comes from the dim outer edges, where the light of what we currently know fades into the blackness of the unknown beyond. James risked his career and his reputation as a scientist to study things that others thought were absurdities. As the president of the American Psychical Society, he seriously and scientifically studied spirits, mediums, and life after death. Most scientists felt this was worthless, but James felt that it was out there on the fringes where we would find new and unexpected vistas of truth.

The tendency of vicious intellectualism stems from a long history of philosophical absolutism - an underlying assumption that there is only one truth. If there is only one truth, then once we find that truth everything else is false. In philosophy, absolutism is the position that there is only one ultimate truth, and even more so, that that truth is valid at all times, in all places, under all circumstances. An opposing point of view is relativism, which holds that there is no absolute truth and that all truth is relative — meaning that it is true only under certain conditions. To give a simple example, imagine being told that John is tall. That might be true compared to the average height of most men, but if you walk into a room where everyone else is taller than John, you would say that John is the short one. Is John tall or short? It depends on the context.

The problem with relativism is that, taken to its extreme, it essentially says that there is no truth. It becomes the nihilistic belief that nothing is true. John, in the example above, is neither tall, nor short. Neither is true about John; they are just words of comparison. If we follow this road all the way to the end, we simply conclude that nothing is ultimately true, which can easily slip into nothing matters. On the other hand, absolutism leads to its own troubles because, in its extreme, it becomes fanaticism that often inspires conflict. Wars have historically been fought when one side believes they are absolutely right and the other is absolutely wrong. If you believe you have found the one and only truth, you will go to any lengths to defend it.

James was not an absolutist. In fact, he's famed for good-naturedly exclaiming, "Damn the absolute!" to one of his colleagues. But he was not a relativist either. He didn't believe that all truth was relative. He did believe that there were truths that were absolutely true, he just believed that there were many of them.

James promoted the position of pluralism. Pluralism is the belief that reality contains more than one fundamental truth. James' belief in pluralism stands in sharp contrast to one of the most foundational pillars of logic — the law of non-contradiction. The law of non-contradiction tells us that no two things can be both true and contradictory. In other words, this animal in front of me can't be both a dog and a cat. The law of non-contradiction leads directly to a tendency toward vicious intellectualism.

James believed that sometimes two things can be both true in an absolute sense and also contradictory. The essential nature of reality is not one, it is many. So, there can be some, and maybe many things, that are absolutely true. Our minds have not been conditioned to think this way. It is very hard for us to imagine that two things can both be absolutely true and contradictory. We can't imagine an animal that is both a cat and a dog at the same time. James felt that, in order for us to grasp the true immensity of reality, we must build the imaginative power necessary to embrace pluralistic thinking. What James was asking us to do was to recognize the realty of paradox and develop a way of thinking that can work with it.

James was often criticized by his peers to be a relativist who did not believe that anything was absolutely true. It was probably inevitable that James' pluralism would attract criticism; after all, it was challenging the philosophical core of the modern world.

For centuries in the classical era of the Western world, God had been assumed to be all-knowing and the word of God, as it was recorded in scripture, was assumed to tell us exactly what was real. The European Enlightenment that propelled us into the modern age was fueled by the recognition that human beings can determine what is true through our own observation and rational thinking. We have the capacity to reason and know what is true for ourselves without needing to rely on the word of God.

This was a liberating leap for humankind that came to be widely recognized as a step into greater maturity as a conscious species. It also left us existentially insecure. Without an all-knowing God to guide us, what were we to trust? The answer we came up with was natural law. Science is based on the premise that the universe is not ruled by God but is governed by universal laws of nature that are immutable and undeniable. Science and its understanding of natural laws became the new source of truth, so much so that saying something was "scientifically proven" became code for saying it was "really true". The seeds of scientism had been planted and it was inevitable that Peirce and James, in proposing a non-material view of reality, would face opposition.

Now that scientists were taking over responsibility for determining what was true, there was an obvious question left open. What exactly would philosophers do?

In the early twentieth century, philosophy took what is now referred to as the "linguistic turn", perhaps in part to distinguish itself from science and remain relevant. During this time, a view spearheaded by thinkers such as Ludwig Wittgenstein, increasingly saw truth as a set of linguistic agreements. And so, philosophers gave up their fascination with the question of "what is real?" and instead started asking, "how do we come to agreements about what is real?"

One of the most influential American philosophers of the second half of the twentieth century was Richard Rorty, who, like James, was deeply concerned with our understanding of truth. Rorty, also like James, was criticized for being a relativist when in fact he was not. Rorty was accused of advocating for the idea that there is no truth, when what he was really saying was that the idea of truth is just not a useful one to hold on to.

In his book *Contingency, Irony and Solidarity*, Rorty lays out a vision of how reality works that builds and expands on James' notion of vicious intellectualism.

When something is contingent, it's dependent on something else. If I say that I will meet with you tomorrow contingent on my not having to work, I'm saying that the truth of my meeting you tomorrow is dependent on me not working. In other words, it is conditional. Rorty's conviction is that all human truth is contingent on the language we have to express it. Claims of truth are made in language, and what we can claim as true is dependent on what our language can describe. To borrow a quote from Wittgenstein, "The limits of my language are the limits of my world."

Rorty is raising some serious questions regarding the universalist belief system of the Enlightenment. In that system, as we have already said, reality is assumed to rest on universal principles and natural laws. We believe that there are essential truths that exist independent of our human understanding of them. In this sense, truth exists out there waiting to be discovered. We have been trained to assume that when we say something is true, we are making a statement about something that exists in reality. This is exactly the idea Rorty asks us to question. Maybe our statements of truth do not reflect reality. Maybe they only tell us what our current language was designed to describe as true. For Rorty, culture doesn't advance as we discover new truths, it advances as we create new languages that can express new truths.

Realty is not discovered; it is created through the literalization of metaphors. Language uses metaphors to express ideas, but over time, we come to believe that the metaphors we make up are communicating real things that exist independently of the metaphors we use to express them. An easy example is the idea of money. Nothing like money actually exists outside of our idea of money and our agreements around that idea.

According to Rorty, we live in a world created by what we can express together in language. We don't live in the world; we live inside of a conversation about the world. And every individual's ultimate reality is defined by what Rorty calls their final vocabulary. A person's final vocabulary is the last set of words they have to define what is real and what really matters. If you take away their final vocabulary, you take away their reality. Our final vocabulary is our ultimate justification; it allows us to believe what we believe for living the way they do.

In his book, Rorty describes two kinds of individuals: ironists and metaphysicians. In doing so, he is attempting to resolve the dilemma of vicious intellectualism that so deeply haunted William James.

An ironist, according to Rorty, is someone who lives with continual doubts about their final vocabulary. They don't trust their understanding of reality and they cannot resolve their doubts with their current language. An ironist doesn't necessarily believe that their final vocabulary is closer to the truth than anyone else's. They are not even sure that there is a final truth that can be expressed in language.

A metaphysician, on the other hand, is someone who believes that there is an ultimate truth and that it can be described in the language they have access to. They develop a final language to express the ultimate truth and they are confident that their final language is closer to the ultimate truth than any other they know of.

In short, the metaphysician is on a quest to find the ultimate theory of everything so that everyone can live by it. The ironist is engaged in a constant act of continually re-describing who they are in the hopes that, by continually shedding any self-created, inherited or imposed ideas, they can live a free and authentic life. The ironist wants to define themselves.

Ironists, as Rorty describes them, reflect an existentialist ideal. Existentialism was another philosophy that came into prominence during the first half of the 20th century.

William Barrett introduced the philosophy of existentialism to American academia with the publication of his book *Irrational*

Man. In the book, he is clear to state that existentialism is strictly a Continental European philosophical movement, although he adds that "of all non-European philosophers William James probably best deserves to be labeled an Existentialist." In fact, Barrett goes so far as to claim that it would be more accurate to call James an existentialist than a pragmatist.

Some existentialists feared that human consciousness had become so dominated by rationalism and materialism that we were rapidly losing our ability to have faith in anything that could not be seen. To some, this appeared to be the road to nihilism, and thinkers like Soren Kierkegaard, Leo Tolstoy and Martin Buber searched for a new footing for spiritual faith in the modern world.

Other existentialists, most notably, Friedrich Nietzsche and Jean-Paul Sartre, felt that we had outgrown the false security that religious belief had granted us and needed to face the emptiness and insecurity of existence. We needed to find a new way to understand meaning, truth and goodness in the vast, unknown and mysterious universe we had found ourselves in.

Both James and Rorty wanted us to embrace the insecurity of realizing that we may never know, and it may not be possible to know, what is true. Both were sometimes accused of being relativists who were courting nihilism. But I think neither of them really were. James, as we have already described, was asking us to embrace a multiplicity of truths. Rorty was asking us to stop worrying about what was truth.

Rorty recognized that the challenge for any ironist was not falling into the trap of attempting to create a universal theory of freedom and authenticity. Any such theory would become just another universal theory that demanded adherence. Rorty simply believed that the idea that there was a truth to be found was just not a useful idea to work with. That didn't mean it wasn't true. It might be true, but even if it were, there would never be any way to be absolutely certain we had found it. The quest for ultimate truth was the source of conflict, division and even war, as sides form around their final vocabularies.

Rorty believed that we should give up our obsession with finding the truth and instead work toward increasing human solidarity.

Rather than creating ideas that match reality, we should create ideas that bring more people closer together.

In a way that is reminiscent of James, Rorty believed that rigid adherence to any idea that we know what is true stifles our creativity, because when we think we already know what is true, our minds tend to close down and we feel little compulsion to look further. Rorty believed the most precious thing we have is our imagination and the more unbridle it is, the better. Peirce's motto, "Never block the road to inquiry," found a good home in Rorty.

Rorty is considered to be the philosopher who revitalized the philosophy of pragmatism after it had all but disappeared from academia after the Second World War. But, between Peirce and James at the start of pragmatism, and Rorty in our own time, there was John Dewey. Dewey was perhaps the most important American philosopher of the 20th century. He is considered to be the third founder of pragmatism and he applied this new thinking about reality sociologically and culturally, in ways that made him one of the primary architects of modern American life. We will explore Dewey and his influence in the next chapter.

CHAPTER TEN

Education for an Evolving Future

John Dewey was the most influential American philosopher of the 20th century. He was born in Burlington, Vermont, in 1859; the same year that Charles Darwin published *On the Origin of Species.* Dewey was introduced to Darwin's book as an undergraduate at the University of Vermont. At this early point, he had an insight about evolution that would guide his thinking throughout his long career.

What Dewey realized was that human beings are part of an evolutionary process that only had one value. The only thing that the process of evolution would ever reward us with was the opportunity for more evolution. Any time a species came to a place where no more evolution was possible, it fell into extinction.

Dewey is sometimes referred to as the father of progressive education because of the tremendous influence he had in updating the school system of the United States. We will not need to look far to see how his insight about evolution became the basis for the education that all American children receive.

In his book *Democracy and Education*, he challenges our common idea of maturity. Generally, we think of growth as a journey that takes us from a state of immaturity to a state of maturity, and the process of maturing is complete when no more growth is needed. The goal of growth seems to be to come to a state where growth can stop. But according to the evidence of evolution, this couldn't be so. We live in a universe that never stops growing, therefore the process of growth cannot lead to the end of growth. The purpose of growth has to be more growth, not less. Our educational system must do more than teach facts and skills; it has to teach us how to learn more and better. The fundamental premise of progressive education is that the goal of education is to learn how to learn.

More generally, Dewey is saying that the process of growth is not taking us from a place of deficiency to a place of fullness. A child is not partial and an adult whole; a child is whole as well. We are never less than whole; we begin whole and we remain whole at every stage of our evolution. Our journey is not from deficiency to wholeness. We are not partial and become whole. We grow from fullness to fullness, whole and complete at every step of the way. Like all of the philosophers we have explored so far in this book, Dewey is committed to a vision of a universe that evolves as a continuous unbroken whole.

Dewey spent a great deal of time thinking about psychology, and in fact, he was deeply influenced by William James' masterwork *The Principles of Psychology*. Dewey's thoughts about human behavior give us a perfect window into his holistic view of reality.

Dewey challenged the idea that human behavior could be adequately explained in terms of stimulus and response. The classic stimulus/response scenario involves some stimulus that spurs a person into action. For instance, the presence of a lion results in a person running. We can quickly see the inadequacy of the stimulus/response explanation if we consider that in a zoo, you can have the same stimulus — a lion — but the environment in which you see the lion changes the response. And if you are in the wild and you are hunting for lions, the same stimulus will create a different response. The overly simplistic stimulus/response explanation doesn't take into account the circumstances in which the stimulus and the response are occurring. You can't separate the stimulus from either the external environment (i.e., being in a zoo) or the mental environment (i.e., the mental state of a hunter vs. a tourist).

The term "stimulus" and the term "response" do not refer to one single thing and one resulting action, they both refer to intricate sets of processes. The stimulus is not "the lion". It is the intricate set of visual images, sights, sounds, mental images, thoughts, understandings, motivations, memories, emotional sensations, physical sensations, muscular movements, etc., that make up the experience of that particular lion at that particular moment in exactly that setting. The "response" is the intricate set of visual images, sights, sounds, mental images, thoughts, understandings, motivations, memories, emotional sensations, physical sensations, muscular movements, etc., that result from seeing the lion.

The so-called stimulus and the so-called response are both made up of intricate sets of visual images, sights, sounds, mental images, thoughts, understandings, motivations, memories, emotional sensations, physical sensations, muscular movements, etc. The fact that there is any boundary between the stimulus and the response is only a matter of interpretation by an observer. If we use the metaphor of currents in the ocean, the "current" and the "ocean" are interpretations of qualities of water. There is no clear line that separates the current from the ocean, just like there is no clear line that separates the stimulus from the response.

This may seem abstract, but I believe that it creates the foundation for a view of reality that is deeply compelling. Dewey is describing all of reality as a constant process of interaction, but not simply the interactions of separate parts of reality. Dewey refuses to chop the universe up into neat parts like stimulus and response. The truth of how human beings interact with the environment is much more intricate, overlapped, interweaved, and endless.

Thought, activity and environment can best be thought of as a constantly interacting circuit; or a single mind of which what you have come to see as "your mind" is one aspect. Imagine what happens when you walk into a room. Your mind moves through different thoughts, feelings, memories, desires, intentions and interests. Your eyes pass over and focus on different aspects of the scene in front of you. If you decide to pick up a book in the room, you will simply think that you did it because you wanted to, without thinking about how the choice to pick up the book actually came about. Perhaps if the book on the table hadn't reminded you of one from your childhood, you would never have picked it up. Maybe you walk into the kitchen and pick up a banana because, unconsciously, you were feeling hungry without yet knowing it. Or you walk into another room and turn on the lamp without realizing that you had unconsciously seen a letter on the desk.

Our thoughts, preferences, ideas, feelings and intentions are constantly interacting with everything around us — both consciously and unconsciously. When we say that we decided to pick up the book or the banana, or turn on the lamp, we are oversimplifying what, in reality, is an intricate set of interacting influences; a process that resulted in picking up the book or the banana, or turning on the lamp. Rather than thinking about people as if they are things that decide to act, Dewey preferred to describe us as a complex flow of activity in constant contact and interaction with the environment. We are a process of perception and activity that constantly alters the environment that we are in. And, in turn, the environment is always affecting and changing us. There is a continuous non-verbal communication occurring between mind, body and environment maintained in a state of dynamic equilibrium. This process of communication can be seen as a higher form of mind.

In his book, *Experience and Nature*, Dewey described nature as an "affair of affairs", and by that he meant that it is a process containing other processes. Our experience of reality tends to be dominated by what appears to be discrete and separate things. Dewey taught people to see these things not as separate, but as the ends of historical events. Everything we see exists as the end product of some process. "Ends" have a unique quality to them. When a succession of events culminates in some final moment, like a cake that comes out of the oven, that moment of completion has the feeling of a termination; an end point that has a quality of finality. The ending might be a happy ending or a bad ending, but either way it feels final.

The esthetic quality of endings tends to grab our attention. In the flow of ongoing activity, the endpoints stand out and get noticed against the blurry background of ongoing process. So, we perceive the endpoints as if they were the reality, but Dewey points out that every end is the completion of a history of events, and it is the beginning of a new history. Reality is one flowing river, a history of histories. Because we are mesmerized by the endpoints, we miss the continuity inherent in the flow. It is like being captivated by the shimmering sparkles on the surface of a river and missing the fact that the river is flowing.

The source of philosophical enlightenment, according to Dewey, is the direct recognition that reality is a flow of incessant beginnings and endings. Everything is constantly emerging out of what happened before in a never-ending stream of becoming. The recognition that reality is an ongoing creative flow is the foundation of the metaphysics of pragmatism.

This brings up one of my fondest childhood memories. I was having dinner with my family at the end of a wonderful day at an amusement park. I only remember the end of that day, sitting at a booth in a restaurant having just eaten dinner. That moment was the end of the history of that day at the park. The history of that day was part of the history of my summer vacation. The history of that vacation was part of the history of my life. My life is part of the history of my generation. The history of my generation is part of the history of America. The history of America is… you can keep going until you see that everything is part of the history of this universe. We don't generally perceive this vast "affair of affairs;" we tend to be focused on just the end in front of us, sitting at a booth in a restaurant having just eaten dinner.

Embracing the continuity of time is central to the pragmatist's view of reality. Everything is in a state of transition between what has been and what will be. Nothing is fixed or settled, everything is constantly in motion. According to Dewey, the reason we don't see the relentless flux and flow of reality is because it is simply too unstable, insecure and scary. Throughout our history, we have celebrated "ends" because they represent stability. There is a feast when the hunt is complete. There is a party after the end of another year of life. Endpoints give us a sense of safety. In a universe of constant flux, we look for things that appear static enough to anchor to. For centuries, the ultimate anchor was the belief in an unchanging god. No matter how crazy things got here on earth, there was always a god in the sky who never wavered.

Nature is a collection of histories and these histories do come to ends, but every end is also a beginning. By recognizing that everything is not only an endpoint but also a beginning, Dewey hoped that we could develop a completely new perception: the ability to see the future in the present. If I look at the wooden table I am working on, I can fairly readily see that it is the end of a history that started as a seed, that grew into a tree, that was cut down, and then turned into a table. But this table is also part of a future history of whatever happens on it, including writing this book.

If we break the habit of seeing everything in terms of the ends of histories, and accept the transitory nature of reality, we will see that everything is in a state of constant "becoming". This opens up the possibility that our awareness will shift from predominantly seeing only the present and past state of things, to a new vision in which the future possibilities of things will become more apparent to us. When we embrace constant flux, future possibilities start to enter into our immediate experience of the present. We begin to intuit the future in the present. In this way, our experience of reality will expand beyond the habit of seeing a static collection of things, or the ends of a history. We would begin to see the entire flow of time in our experience of the present.

The beautiful image that develops in *Experience and Nature* is a vision of reality as an ocean of mind. Think of the mind as an ocean, and within that ocean, there are currents. Now, imagine that there are objects floating on the surface of the ocean. The objects represent people, and the direction that the objects will float in over the surface of the ocean will be determined by which current they get caught in.

Objects in the ocean get swept into one current and carried along for a while in that direction. Then another current picks them up and sweeps them off in a different direction. Different objects get swept along by different currents, in different directions, and as the currents change, the movement of the objects also change.

If you look at the ocean, you don't see the currents in it directly, what you see are patterns in the motion of objects floating on the surface of the water. To use another example, you don't see a magnetic field directly, but if you pour iron filings on the table around the magnet, the filings will arrange themselves along lines of force that you can then see.

The mind is also not something you can see directly, and Dewey did not believe that it was something that exists in our heads. It is more like an ocean with currents, or a magnetic field with lines of force. We only see the currents in the ocean of mind by seeing the direction that people's thoughts and actions take. When you see someone going to work every day, you realize that "going to work every day" is a current in the ocean of mind that many people are caught in. Other patterns of human behavior reveal other currents in the ocean of mind that we live in.

Dewey thought of the currents of mind as ideas that act like signs or pointers that direct us toward specific possibilities. The idea of "having a job" points to a way of life that involves going to work every day. The idea of "responsibility for your family" is another current that might reinforce the current of "having a job". Ideas are currents in the ocean of mind. Ideas have energy in them. If you hold onto an idea long enough, it will sweep you up and lead you to take certain actions that will bring you, inevitably, into certain future possibilities.

Look at all of the ideas that you hold and notice the energy they have. They point towards, and sometimes even compel us towards, different possible futures. Allow yourself to get a sense of the fluid liquid ocean of ideas that we are all swimming in. Get a sense of how it is sweeping you along, pushing you in this direction, carrying you in that one. We are like objects floating in an ocean of ideas, but we are not passive. We create the ideas and adjust the ideas. We change our minds; we have some ideas that tell us to do one thing, other ideas that tell us to do the opposite, and still other ideas that help us decide between the two. Currents of mind carry us along, but we can also alter the currents and affect our destiny. By changing our ideas, we alter the path that our energy and our actions will follow. Changing our ideas changes the future.

Dewey wanted to use ideas to change culture because culture is such an important container that directs the flow of human activity. Ideas compel us toward future possibilities. A culture is a collection of ideas whose meaning is held in common by a given group of people. These ideas direct the flow of all the human energy and activity in that culture, and lead the culture as a whole toward specific futures.

There is one profound difficulty in this theory of cultural evolution: How do you decide what direction culture should follow? Adolf Hitler was masterful at directing the flow of energy and activity of people in the direction he wanted to manifest. Unfortunately, the results of his efforts were horrific. The lack of a clear moral foundation for pragmatic thinking was a problem that preoccupied all of the three founders of that philosophy.

Dewey realized, early on in his intellectual career, that the process of evolution only rewards the potential for still greater evolution. Anytime the direction of evolution becomes stifling to the possibility of further growth, the process changes course in search of expansive opportunities. Avenues that hold no promise for expansion are left to atrophy and wither. The moral good would then have to be in whatever direction leads to the greatest possibility for further growth and evolution.

Attempts to create an ethics based on evolution have been tried before Dewey. Those efforts had proven unsatisfactory at best, and led to disturbing notions such as Social Darwinism at worst. Dewey believed that these failures resulted from applying evolution to ethics without letting go of the preference for ends. Any evolutionary ethics that defines "goodness" in terms of some perfected state or endpoint, misses completely the purpose of evolution because evolution isn't headed toward a perfect state. Evolution moves forward in ways that simultaneously bring resolution to problems of the past and create new complexities that will only be resolved with further evolution. If we expect to arrive at some perfected state, we will find ourselves frustrated by what appears to be our perpetual lack of progress.

Goodness in an evolving universe will never be found in the experience of moving closer to a goal. It is experienced as the feeling of growth in the present moment. Goodness is not a goal that exists in the future; it is the act of evolving, perfecting and moving forward. It means moving into experiences with more meaning and significance. We must give up our concern with some imagined perfect future and find our moral compass in a sense of favorable expansion — or, we could say, Evolutionary Love — that can only be found right here in our experience of the present moment.

We have learned to navigate into the future by imagining the best possible end results of our actions and then working toward them. This means the future we are working toward will always be limited by what we can imagine now. Dewey didn't believe that the future exists later; the future exists now because time is a continuous whole and nothing separates the present from the future. We can learn to perceive the future directly in the present. We can learn to perceive future possibilities as they exist right now; that is, as faint whispers in our current experience. We can learn how to discern which future possibility contains more evolutionary potency and possibility. In this way, we can stop being guided by our ideas about the future and start to be guided by our experience of it in the present.

Dewey was a socially engaged philosopher. He worked closely with the famous activist and social reformer Jane Addams, who was the first American woman to be awarded a Nobel Peace Prize. Dewey was involved with the early version of the National Association for the Advancement of Colored People (NAACP), and he directed the famous Dewey Commission that cleared Leon Trotsky of the charges levied against him by Joseph Stalin. Dewey was committed to the advancement of American culture, and he believed the way to accomplish this was to seed the culture with the big and important ideas that would direct the activities of everyone in that culture. The ideas of education, freedom and democracy occupied Dewey during his entire life, and his writings had a profound shaping influence on American life throughout the 20th century.

In the 1860's, Charles Sanders Peirce and William James met together as part of the Metaphysical Club and discussed the ideas that would later develop into the philosophy of pragmatism. That philosophy, rooted in the belief that the value of an idea had to be proven in action, would become a powerful force in world philosophy during the early decades of the twentieth century. Then the First World War erupted, followed by the Great Depression, and later the rise to power of the Third Reich and the horror of the Second World War.

With these events, the progressive spirit of modernism — of which pragmatism was surely a part — took a hard hit. After all, these events, and especially the rise of Nazi Germany, happened in fully modern countries utilizing modern technology and modern ideas. Progressive ideas began to fall out of favor and many people began to believe that overemphasizing progress would inevitably result in a loss of deeper human values.

At Columbia University, Dewey, who was the chair of the philosophy department, found himself intellectually opposed by a new movement, traditionalism. Traditionalist colleagues of Dewey's, like Mortimer Adler and Mark Van Doren, were teaching their students to look toward the great literary works of human history to rediscover and reclaim the deep truths and spiritual values that we had lost.

Mark Van Doren taught literature at Columbia and was so beloved by his students that there is, to this day, a Mark Van Doren award given for teaching excellence. He had a unique ability to infuse his students with an appreciation of the depth and beauty that could be found in the great writings of humanity. And fueled by his guidance and inspiration, three of his students would go on to play significant roles in creating a new cultural movement that would challenge the progressive mood of Modernism. These young students of Van Doren's were all looking for deeper spiritual meaning in a world that they saw as desperately in need of an awakening. These three students were Thomas Merton, Allen Ginsberg and Jack Kerouac.

Merton would pursue spirit as a Catholic monk, and gain fame as an enormously popular author and pioneer of interfaith dialogue through his historic meetings with Asian spiritual masters.

Ginsberg and Kerouac hunted spiritual revelation through poetry, prose, drugs, alcohol and Buddhism. They ignited the Beat movement as writers and poets in the 1950s, which in turn, catalyzed the counterculture hippie movement of the 1960s that eventually gave birth to the New Age spirituality of the seventies and eighties.

Politically and economically, the progressive side of modernity also came under attack. As the American version of democracy and the free market economy began to show its blemishes, many turned to socialism and communism for answers. Philosophy, too, saw a turning away from the future-oriented passion of pragmatism, with its optimistic view of human progress, toward a more skeptical mood in which the idea that *truth could be conveyed in language* became suspect.

All of these leanings and tendencies were part of what is sometimes seen as the cultural shift into a postmodern worldview. Postmodernism is impossible to define in any simple way, and means many different things in different contexts. For our purposes, we could characterize it as a cultural backlash against the shortcomings of modernism, and say that pragmatism was one of its victims. Pragmatism, in the middle of the 20th century, had disappeared almost entirely from university philosophy departments. That is, until Richard Rorty revived interest in pragmatism, first through the groundbreaking publication of his book *Philosophy and the Mirror of Nature*, and then with his famous public disagreements with another prominent American philosopher Hilary Putnam.

The rebirth of interest in progressive philosophy seems to be evident in the many forms of evolutionary spirituality growing in popularity today. There seems to be increasing willingness to trust a wholehearted embrace of the power of human creativity. Perhaps the ideas of classical American philosophers like Emerson, Peirce, James and Dewey will find their way back into the public's eye.

I believe there is an authentic American enlightenment tradition to be found in the ideas of American philosophy and I hope that this book inspires you to explore them more deeply.

Apel, Karl-Otto. *Charles S. Peirce: From Pragmatism to Pragmaticism.* Translated by John Michael Krois, University of Massachusetts Press, 1981.

Barrett, William. *Irrational Man: A Study in Existential Philosophy.* Anchor Books, 1990.

Berlin, Isaiah. *The Roots of Romanticism.* Princeton University Press, 2013.

Bernstein, Richard J. *The Pragmatic Turn.* Polity, 2010.

Brandom, Robert B. *Reason in Philosophy: Animating Ideas.* Harvard University Press, 2013.

Coleridge, Samuel Taylor. *Aids to Reflection and the confessions of an Inquiring Spirit.* George Bell and Sons, 1901.

Cooke, George Willis. *Ralph Waldo Emerson: His Life, Writings, and Philosophy.* Boston, 1882.

Dewey, John. *Experience and Nature.* Courier Corporation, 1958.

Emerson, Ralph Waldo. *History.* 1841. ARC Manor, 2007.

Emerson, Ralph Waldo. *Nature.* Boston, 1836.

Emerson, Ralph Waldo. *Nominalist and Realist.* Boston, 1844.

Emerson, Ralph Waldo. *Representative Men.* Boston,1850.

Emerson, Ralph Waldo. *The Conduct of Life*, Boston, 1860.

Emerson, Ralph Waldo. *The Over-Soul.* Boston, 1841.

Emerson, Ralph Waldo. "American Scholar Address." Phi Beta Kappa Society, August 31, 1837, Harvard College, Cambridge, MA. Speech.

Emerson, Ralph Waldo. "Divinity School Address." Harvard Divinity School graduation, July 15, 1838, Harvard Divinity School, Cambridge, MA. Speech.

Emerson, Ralph Waldo. "Fate." *The Conduct of Life*, Boston, 1860.

Gura, Philip F. *American Transcendentalism: A History*. Hill and Wang, 2008.

Hausman, Carl R. *Charles S. Peirce's Evolutionary Philosophy*. Cambridge University Press, 1993.

Houser, Nathan, and Kloesel, Christian, editors. *The Essential Peirce: Selected Philosophical Writings,* vol. 1. Indiana University Press, 1992.

James, William. *The Principles of Psychology*. New York, Henry Holt, 1890.

James, William. *The Varieties of Religious Experience*. Longmans, Green & Co., 1902.

James, William. *The Will to Believe*. 1896. Arterna Classics, 2018.

James, William. "Are we Automata?" Mind, vol. 4, 1879, pp. 1-22.

James, William. "A World of Pure Experience." *The Journal of Philosophy, Psychology, and Scientific Method*, vol. 1, no. 20, 1904, pp. 533-543.

Kant, Immanuel. *Kant: Critique of Pure Reason*. Translated and edited by Paul Guyer and Allen W. Wood, Cambridge University Press, 1999.

Margolis, Joseph. *Reinventing Pragmatism: American Philosophy at the End of the Twentieth Century*. Cornell University Press, 2002.

Margolis, Joseph. *The Unraveling of Scientism: American Philosophy at the End of the Twentieth Century*. Cornell University Press, 2003.

Peirce, Charles S. "Design and Chance." *Writings of Charles S. Peirce: A chronological Edition*, vol. 4, Indiana University Press, 1989.

Peirce, Charles S. "Evolutionary Love." *The Monist*, vol. 3, no. 2, 1893, pp. 176-200.

Peirce, Charles S. "The Architecture of Theories." *The Monist*, vol. 1, no. 2, 1891, pp. 161-176.

Richardson, Robert D. *William James: In the Maelstrom of American Modernism*. Houghton Mifflin Company, 2007.

Richardson Jr., Robert D. *Emerson: The Mind on Fire*. University of California Press, 1996.

Rorty, Richard. *Contingency, Irony, and Solidarity*. Cambridge University Press, 1989.

Rorty, Richard. *Philosophy and the Mirror of Nature*. Princeton University Press, 1979.

Schopenhauer, Arthur. *The World as Will and Idea*. 7th ed., translated by R. B Haldane & J. Kemp; Kagan Paul, Trench, Trübner & Co., 1909.

Sheriff, John. K. *Charles Peirce's Guess at the Riddle*. Indiana University Press, 1994.

Steiner, Rudolf. *The Theory of Knowledge Implicit in Goethe's Conception*. Translated by Olin D. Wannamaker. Dornach, 1886.

Jeff Carreira is a meditation teacher, mystical philosopher and author who teaches to a growing number of people throughout the world. As a teacher, Jeff offers retreats and courses guiding individuals in a form of meditation he refers to as The Art of Conscious Contentment. Through this simple and effective meditation technique, Jeff has led thousands of people in the journey beyond the confines of fear and self-concern into the expansive liberated awareness that is our true home.

As a philosopher, Jeff is interested in defining a new way of being in the world that will move us from our current paradigm of separation and isolation into an emerging paradigm of unity and wholeness. He is exploring some of the most revolutionary ideas and systems of thought in the domains of spirituality, consciousness, and human development. He leads courses in this new understanding of reality and teaches people how to question their experience until previously held assumptions about the nature of reality fall away to create the space for a dramatically new understanding to emerge.

Jeff is passionate about philosophy because he is passionate about the power of ideas to shape how we perceive reality and how we live together. His enthusiasm for learning is infectious, and he enjoys addressing student groups and inspiring them to develop their own powers of inquiry. He has taught students at colleges and universities throughout the world.

In a world in which university education is often thought of as a vocational certificate, seeing someone obviously relishing the acquisition and sharing of knowledge for its own sake is inspiring.
—Dr. William O. Shropshire
Provost and Professor Emeritus
Ogelthorpe University

Jeff is the author of numerous books including: *Philosophy Is Not a Luxury, Radical Inclusivity, The Soul of a New Self, Paradigm Shifting, The Art of Conscious Contentment, and The Miracle of Meditation.*

For more information visit: www.jeffcarreira.com

Made in the USA
Columbia, SC
28 December 2020